The World Peace Agenda

Based on Shanti-Parva of the Mahabharata

This book presents Shanti-Parva's peace-messages for consideration by UN, UNESCO, all governments, all religious leaders, and by everyone else, with the hope that plenty of purposeful discussion (with an open mind) will be held, to arrive at new proposals which can help bring world peace within the reach of mankind in the twenty-first century.

Readers will discover that the peace-promoting messages of Shanti-Parva (when suitably interpreted) have universal applicability, even today. These messages envisage the launching of a new peace-initiative, based on the explicit declaration of the Mahabharata verse 12.94.1 that says, "wars cannot provide a satisfactory solution to any dispute", and incorporate several novel features which are summarized in the last chapter of this book.

The World Peace Agenda

Based on Shanti-Parva of the
Mahabharata

SATYA P. AGARWAL
Ph.D. (UC, Berkeley)
Formerly, Chief Technical Adviser,
Specialized Agency (ILO) of the United Nations and
Visiting Scholar,
University of California, Berkeley

New Age Books

ISBN: 978-81-7822-308-7

First Indian Edition: Delhi, 2007

Published by
NEW AGE BOOKS
A-44, Naraina Industrial Area, Phase-I
New Delhi 110 028 (INDIA)
Email: nab@vsnl.in
Website: www.newagebooksindia.com

Distributors
Urmila Agarwal
11293 Ridermark Row
Columbia MD 21044
Tel.: USA-410-997-7175
Email: ishamaya@erols.com

Printed in India
at Shri Jainendra Press
A-45, Naraina Phase-I, New Delhi 110 028

To
My Parents
Who taught me
That knowledge should be used
For the good of the world
i.e. Lokasamgraha

Contents

Humble Submission Regarding the Sanskrit Text

The author asks for forgiveness from the Mahabharata-specialists for not having used the critical edition of the epic. Due to his life-long association with the Editor of Gita Press, Gorakhpur, he has at his finger-tips, the peace-messages extracted from their six-volume (unabridged) version, and he feels that the use of the critical edition would probably have no significant impact on these messages.

Secondly, the author asks for forgiveness from specialists in linguistics for not having strictly adhered to all the rules of transliteration. Similarly, he has not given a word-for-word translation of the selected verses. He feels that the purpose of this book will be better served by giving priority to the convenience of general readers.

Thirdly, the author asks for forgiveness from specialists in absolute non-violence for not having restricted the presentation to non-militaristic messages only. These specialists might feel relieved to know that the author has faithfully enumerated the Mahabharata's messages of peace, in which the share of the non-violence based messages can (if necessary) be estimated to be approximately 96 per cent (this last figure being mentioned to satisfy the demand of 21st century scholars who prefer to have quantitative estimates to the maximum extent possible).

Acknowledgements

My plan to write this book took a concrete shape when Dr. S.N. Dwivedi, President of WAVES (World Association for Vedic Studies) asked for my active participation in the International Conference on Global Harmony and Peace, that was organized by WAVES and held at the University of Houston in July 2006. Because of the inspiration that this conference generated and which became instrumental in getting this work started, I want to express my special thanks to Dr. Dwivedi. I was assigned chairmanship of the session on Practical Steps to World Peace, and I am grateful to the peace-promoting scholars who presented thought-provoking papers at that session, viz. Patricia Keefe, Himendra Thakur, Dr. Radhey Shyam Dwivedi, and Anil Narang. I also want to thank Dr. Shashi Tiwari, Dr. Mahavir and Dr. Anuradha Anand who took special interest in the message of world peace that I had extracted from the Mahabharata and which provided the conceptual base, offering immense scope for expansion, ultimately taking the form of the present book.

Members of my family provided constant and substantive support without which I could not possibly have completed the writing of this book. My wife Urmila played a unique role as a joint decision-maker on the approach to be adopted, and she also visualized the cover design. Our children and their spouses, and our grandchildren (viz. Nishkam, Kokila, Seema, David, Isha, Kiran, Priya, Maya) were always keen as well as competent to ensure the successful conclusion of the project. Technical and moral support was spontaneously given by close friends and members of our extended family, viz. Shri Harish Kashyap, M.M. Agarwal, Abhay Bhushan, Rakesh and Alka Mital, Shri Gulab Khandelwal, Dr. K.M. Mital, Renu Mital, Arun and Ritu Gupta, Veena and Anil Kumar, Manju and Dhanendra Kumar, Shreekanta Nayak, Dr. B.P. Shah, Dr. Pramud Rawat, Jaishriben, Veerbalaben, Ila Desai, Shri Mahendrabhai Jhaveri, Dr. Pooran and Kusum Shukla, Rakshpal and Santosh Aggarwal, Dr. Sham Narula, Dr. Dinesh Sinha, and Sarita and Anil Agarwal. Words cannot adequately express the feeling of indebtedness that I have towards all of them (as well as many others whose names are not specifically mentioned because of the need to keep the list short). The responsibility for the views expressed in this book is, however, entirely my own, and not of any of the above-mentioned persons.

New Year Day
1-1-2007

Satya P. Agarwal

CHAPTER 1

The Purpose and Plan of the Book

1.1. This book is the latest output of a twenty-year-old (and still continuing) research project. In 1986, when the author retired from UN, he started a family-supported study of ancient Sanskrit texts (mainly Bhagavad-Gita and Mahabharata) with focus on lokasamgraha (good of the world). In 1992, this study got elevated to a university-based Individual Research Project because the University of California, Berkeley, appointed him Visiting Scholar at the Center for South Asia Studies. Academically, the pursuit and direction of research as well as the quality of its output, continued to be the author's responsibility. In July 2006, the author's active participation in an international conference on world peace,[1] held at the University of Houston, helped shift the focus of research, from lokasamgraha to world peace, or rather to an amalgamation of the two inter-related concepts. The present book is the latest entity in the series of publications through which the findings of the research project (all aimed at serving mankind) have been made available to the citizens of the world.

1.2. The purpose of this book is to bring together nearly one hundred messages of peace, from four inter-related sources, viz. Vedas, Upanisads, Bhagavad-Gita and Mahabharata. Of course, most of the messages are from the Mahabharata, because it has a large section (Shanti-Parva) specifically devoted to peace. Although common people generally view the Mahabharata as a book of war, yet scholars know that more than fifty percent of this book (which is the longest book of the ancient world) deals with lokasamgraha as well as world peace. The Mahabharata's approach, recommending a joint look at lokasamgraha and world peace, gives a clear message that the biggest contribution to world peace can be made only by those governments which follow lokasamgraha-policies within their own respective countries. The implication of this for the author is that the present book, together with his earlier (ten) books,[2] thus form a unified series.

1.3. As to the plan of the book, chapters two, three, and four, are devoted (one each) to the Vedas, the Upanisads, and the Bhagavad-Gita, respectively. Thereafter, chapter five presents Mahabharata's elaboration and extension of Bhagavad-Gita's ideas (mainly on lokasamgraha). The next three chapters (*i.e.* chapters 6-7-8) contain Mahabharata's messages for consideration by (a) governments, (b) religious leaders, and (c) everyone else—this three-fold classification being a true reflection of a three-part composition of Shanti-Parva itself. Finally, chapter nine has a consolidated summary of the peace-messages, and it ends with concluding remarks about the likely follow-up of the messages.

1.4. The title of the book "World Peace Agenda" makes it clear that the messages presented therein are in the nature of a draft for discussion. It is hoped that plenty of purposeful discussion (with an open mind) will be held all over the world, by governments, religious leaders, NGOs, UNESCO, and UN, to arrrive at new proposals which can help bring world peace within the reach of mankind, in the twenty-first century.

CHAPTER 2

The Vedic Message of Peace

2.1. The Vedic message of peace is a socio-religious message, with two components:

(a) Social relationship component

(b) Religion-related component.

The write-up in the present chapter can be viewed as a "twenty-first century interpretation of the Vedic message", to distinguish it from the interpretations put forward by other scholars in earlier centuries. In our opinion, both the social and religious components of this message need to be presented in the most acceptable (universal) form because the purpose is to make a useful contribution to the cause of world peace. More specifically, the social component need not be weakened by the social stratification scheme contained in the Vedas. In other words, the Vedic appeal for promoting "freely chosen social cohesion" need not be diluted by mingling therewith the historical fact that the Vedic society had four varnas or groups (viz. brahmin, ksatriya, vaisya, and sudra). Similarly, the religious component need not be weakened by the possible existence of polytheistic ideas in some sections of the Vedas. In other words, the Vedic statement: "Reality is One", need not be diluted by mingling therewith the textual evidence about many of the Vedic hymns having been addressed to Indra, Agni, Varuna, and other deities (Vedas themselves have clarified this, as we shall explain when we arrive at the relevant section).

2.2. There is one more clarification to be made about the distinguishing feature of our presentation. For this purpose, we need to make a brief mention of what can be called a "prayer-oriented message of peace". Organisations giving such a message have stated that prayers using Gayatri Mantra of the Vedas can contribute to world peace. Similarly, some organisations have stated that prayers using 'Shanti-patha' of the Vedas can contribute to world peace. We will write about Gayatri Mantra and Shanti-patha when we make use of those hymns as a part of our own interpretation. The clarification to be made now is that our presentation can be called an "action-oriented message of peace", to distinguish it from a "prayer-oriented message of peace".

Vedic Message of Peace Expressed in the Terminology of Social Relationships

2.3. The Vedas appealed for "freely chosen social cohesion, in the interest of happiness of all". Eight points of this appeal are particularly important.

2.4. All the members of the society were advised to cultivate an attitude of togetherness. Rigveda first gave such a message, and then Atharvaveda repeated it.

2.5. सं गच्छध्वं सं वदध्वं
सं वो मनांसि जानताम् ।
देवा भागं यथा पूर्वे
सं जनाना उपासते ॥ ऋ० 10.191.2

sangacchadhvam saṁvadadhvam
saṁvo manāṁsi jānatām
devā bhāgaṁ yathā pūrve
sanjanānā upāsate —*Rigveda* 10.191.2

Simple meaning—Move ahead, together. Speak in one sweet voice. May you all have similar, meaningful aspirations. Follow the path illumined by exemplary persons who came before you—they performed their own duty nicely, and you should do likewise.

2.6. सं जानीध्वं सं पृच्यध्वं
सं वो मनांसि जानताम् ।
देवा भागं यथा पूर्वे
सं जनाना उपासते ॥ अ० 6. 64.1

sanjānīdhvaṁ saṁpricyadhvam
saṁvo manāṁsi jānatām
devā bhāgam yathā pūrve
sanjanānā upāsate —*Atharvaveda* 6.64.1

Simple meaning—Together, you should acquire right knowledge. Live in harmony. May you all have similar, meaningful aspirations. Follow the path illumined by exemplary persons who came before you—they performed their own duty nicely, and you should do likewise.

2.7. Use of sweet and truthful words was to go hand-in-hand with togetherness. Again, both Rigveda and Atharvaveda gave the messages that are presented here.

निर्दुरर्मण्य ऊर्जा मधुमती वाक् ।
मधुमती स्थ मधुमतीं वाचमुदेयम् ॥ अ० 16.2.1-2

nirdurarmaṇya ūrjā madhumati vāk
madhumatī stha madhumatīṁ vācamudeyam
—*Atharvaveda* 16.2.1-2

Simple meaning—Nurture sweet ideas, free from evil thoughts.Use sweet words, hear sweet words.

2.8. ऋतावान ऋतजाता ऋतावृधो
घोरासो अनृतद्विषः ।
तेषां वः सुम्ने सुच्छर्दिष्टमे
नरः स्याम ये च सूरयः ॥ ऋ० 7.66.13

ritāvāna ritajātā ritāvridho
ghorāso anritadviṣaḥ
teṣāṁ vaḥ sumne succhardiṣṭame
naraḥ syāma ye ca sūrayaḥ —*Rigveda* 7.66.13

Simple meaning—Listen, O speakers of truth, your life is committed to truth, your effort is committed to truth. Untruth will stay far from you. We, common people, want to follow you. We, educated people, also want to follow you.

2.9. It was important to keep away, feelings of rivalry or dislike or cruelty, and this was to be achieved by means of right knowledge and determined effort for purification of mind. All the four Vedas gave such a message (although the hymns presented here are from three of them, viz. Rigveda, Samaveda, and Atharvaveda).

2.10. यदिह घोरं यदिह क्रूरं यदिह पापं
तच्छान्तं तच्छिवं सर्वमेव शमस्तु नः। अ. 19.9.14

yadiha ghoraṁ yadiha krūraṁ yadiha pāpaṁ
tacchāntaṁ tacchivaṁ sarvameva shamastu naḥ
—*Atharvaveda* 19.9.14

Simple meaning—Whatever is harsh, may that become peaceful. Whatever is cruel, may that become kind. Whatever is unrighteous, may that become purified. May all achieve peace. May none be put to harm.

This hymn forms a part of Shānti-patha (or rather a detailed version thereof. We want to clarify that a shorter version of Shanti-patha is also in use). Readers may like to refer to para 2.2 about the role of Shanti-patha in a "prayer-oriented message of peace." (Also please see para 2.66)

2.11. नकिर्देवा मिनीमसि नकिरायोपयामसि
मन्त्रश्रुत्यं चरामसि।
पक्षेभिरपि कक्षेभिरत्राभि संरभामहे॥ ऋ. 10.134.7

nakirdevā minīmasi nakirāyopayāmasi
mantrashrutyam carāmasi
pakṣebhirapi kakṣebhiratrābhi saṁrabhāmahe
—*Rigveda* 10.134.7

Simple meaning—O God, we assure you that we do not commit violence against any human being, nor do we cause conflict in the society. Our conduct is in accordance with Vedic hymns. In our eyes, none is small, none is big. All of us act together.

2.12. सोम : पवते जनिता मतीनां
जनिता दिवो जनिता पृथिव्या : ।
जनिताग्नेर्जनिता सूर्यस्य
जनितेन्द्रस्य जनितोत विष्णोः ॥ सा: 6.4.3

somaḥ pavate janitā matīnāṁ
janitā divo janitā prithivyāḥ
janitāgnerjanitā sūryasya
janitendrasya janitota viṣnoḥ —*Samaveda* 6.4.3

Simple meaning—O God, you are the purifier, you are the giver of prosperity. Vedas came from you, all the worlds came from you. All energy (sun, moon, fire) came from you. Indra came from you. Vishnu came from you.

2.13. अभयं न : करत्यन्तरिक्षमभयं
द्यावापृथिवी उभे इमे ।
अभयं पश्चादभयं पुरस्ताद्
उत्तरादधरादभयं नो अस्तु ॥ अ० 19.15.5

abhayaṁ naḥ karatyantarikshamabhyaṁ
dyāvāprithivī ubhe ime
abhayaṁ pashcādabhayaṁ purastād
uttarādadharādabhayaṁ no astu
—*Atharvaveda* 19.15.5

Simple meaning—O God, make us free from fear. May the sky cause no fear. May the world cause no fear. May no fear come to us from the front, may no fear come to us from the back. May no fear come to us from above, may no fear come to us from below.

2.14. येन देवा न वियंति
नो च विद्विषते मिथः ।
तत्कृण्मो ब्रह्म वो गृहे
संज्ञानं पुरुषेभ्यः ॥ अ० 3.30.4

yena devā na viyanti
no ca vidviṣate mithaḥ

tatkriṇmo brahma vo grihe
sanjñānaṁ puruṣebhyaḥ —*Atharvaveda* 3.30.4

Simple meaning—Listen, all men and women, acquire right knowledge, so that there is no conflict within your homes, so that there is no enmity within your society. Acquire such knowledge.

2.15. ज्यायस्वन्तश्चित्तिनो मा वि यौष्ट
संराधयन्त : सधुराश्चरन्त : ।
अन्यो अन्यस्मै वल्गु वदन्त
एत सध्रीचीनान्वः संमनस्कृणोमि ॥ अ० 3.30.5

jyāyasvantashcittino mā vi yauṣṭa
saṁrādhayantaḥ sadhurāshcarantaḥ
anyo anyasmai valgu vadanta
eta sadhrīcīnānvaḥ saṁmanaskriṇomi
—*Atharvaveda* 3.30.5

Simple meaning—Listen, all men and women, give due respect to elderly members of the society. Let no one feel isolated. Apply your mind to achieve success. Always stay under one umbrella, united. Speak sweetly with one another. Have similar aspirations and cultivate feelings of heart-felt unity. My blessings are with you.

2.16. Food production was to be increased, and through proper distribution and sharing, no one was to be left hungry. Hymns giving this message have been selected from Rigveda and Atharvaveda.

2.17. युनक्त सीरा वि युगा तनुध्वं
कृते योनौ वपतेह बीजम् ।
गिरा च श्रुष्टिः सभरा असन्नो
नेदीय इत्सृण्यः पक्वमेयात् ॥ ऋ० 10.101.3

yunakta sīrā vi yugā tanudhvaṁ
krite yonau vapateha bījaṁ
girā ca shruṣṭiḥ sabharā asanno
nedīya itsriṇyaḥ pakvameyāt
—*Rigveda* 10.101.3

Simple meaning—O farmers, plough the field. Sow the seed when the time is right. When the crop is ready, harvest it and collect the grain properly. Mother earth will give you plenty of food.

2.18. अशितावत्यतिथावश्नीयाद् ।
यज्ञस्य सात्मत्वाय
यज्ञस्याविच्छेदाय
तद् व्रतम् ॥ अ० 9.6.3

ashitāvatyatithāvashnīyād
yajñasya sātmatvāya
yajñasyāvicchedāya
tad vratam —*Atharvaveda* 9.6.3

Simple meaning—Listen, O householders, the food that you have is not only for you, but also for others. In fact, first offer the food to your guests and visitors. Such sharing of food is yajna (sacred act of sacrifice). Maintain such yajna, in the interest of maintaining life on this planet.

2.19. प्रजाभ्य : पुष्टिं विभजन्त आसते ।
रयिमिव पृष्ठं प्रभवंतमायते ॥ ऋ० 2.13.4

prajābhyaḥ puṣṭiṁ vibhajanta āsate
rayimiva priṣṭhaṁ prabhavantamāyate
—*Rigveda* 2.13.4

Simple meaning—O God, you have given food and wealth to us, and you have also given us wisdom to share with others what we have. We feel happy only after we have done such sharing.

2.20. स इद्भोजो यो गृहवे ददाति
अन्नकामाय चरते कृशाय ।
अरमस्मै भवति यामहूता
उतापरीषु कृणुते सखायम् ॥ ऋ० 10.117.3

sa idbhojo yo grihave dadāti
annakāmāya carate krishāya

aramasmai bhavati yāmahūtā
utāparīṣu kriṇute sakhāyam —*Rigveda* 10.117.3

Simple meaning—Listen,O householders, every one eats food, but I want to tell you who eats the right food. Whoever first offers food to those who are hungry and looking for food, that person eats the right food. Furthermore, that person need not worry whether his or her food supply will be adequate—I will give more to that person. Also, such a person will have plenty of helpful friends.

2.21. All efforts were to be made to upgrade the value system of the people in such a way that the well-being of the society (i.e. every one without exception) received priority. All the four Vedas provided inspiration for such efforts (although the hymns presented here are from three of them, viz. Rigveda, Yajurveda and Atharvaveda).

2.22. सहृदयं सांमनस्यं
अविद्वेषं कृणोमि वः ।
अन्यो अन्यमभि हर्यत
वत्सं जातमिवाघ्न्या ॥ अ० 3.30.1

sahridayaṁ sāmmanasyaṁ
avidveṣaṁ kriṇomi vaḥ
anyo anyamabhi haryata
vatsaṁ jātamivāghnyā —*Atharvaveda* 3.30.1

Simple meaning—Listen, O men and women, I am filling your hearts with sympathy so that you will love one another and have no trace of ill-will.

2.23. स्वस्ति मात्र उत पित्रे नो अस्तु ।
स्वस्ति गोभ्यो जगते पुरुषेभ्यः ॥ अ० 1.31.4

svasti mātra uta pitre no astu
svasti gobhyo jagate puruṣebhyaḥ
—*Atharvaveda* 1.31.4

Simple meaning—O God, we pray for the welfare of our mother and father.We also pray for the welfare of our cows. In fact, we pray for the welfare of all beings.

2.24. भद्रं नो अपि वातय मनो
दक्षमुत क्रतुम् ॥ ऋ० 10.25.1

bhadraṁ no api vātaya mano
daksamuta kratum —*Rigveda* 10.25.1

Simple meaning—O God, give us the desire to do good to others, give us also the capability to help others.

2.25. आ नो भद्रा : क्रतवो यन्तु विश्वतो
अदब्धासो अपरितास उद्भिदः ॥ ऋ० 1.89.1

ā no bhadrāḥ kratavo yantu vishvato
adabdhaso aparitāsa udbhidaḥ —*Rigveda* 1.89.1

Simple meaning—O God, bless us so that our welfare-oriented activities may expand world-wide and may become effective, overcoming all obstacles.

2.26. सध्रीचीनान्वः संमनसस्कृणोमि
एकश्नुटीन् संवननेन सर्वान् ।
देवा इवाऽमृतं रक्षमाणाः
सायंप्रातः सौमनसो वो अस्तु ॥ अ० 3.30.7

sadhrīcīnānvaḥ sammanasaskriṇomi
ekashnuṭīn samvananena sarvān
devā ivāmritaṁ raksamāṇāḥ
sāyamprātaḥ saumanaso vo astu —*Atharvaveda* 3.30.7

Simple meaning—Listen, O men and women, my blessings are with you, to strengthen your desire to do good to all. You will move forward, together, sharing joys and sorrows. Just as great leaders doing good to all enjoyed bliss, you too will enjoy bliss, at all times.

2.27. भूर्भुवः स्वः तत्सवितुर्वरेण्यं
भर्गो देवस्य धीमहि ।
धियो यो नः प्रचोदयात् ॥ य० 36.3

bhūrbhuvaḥ svaḥ tatsaviturvarenyaṁ
bhargo devasya dhīmahi
dhiyo yo naḥ pracodayāt —*Yajurveda* 36.3

Simple meaning—This is Gayatri Mantra, the most famous hymn of the Vedas. Through this hymn, all the members of the society pray for the right value system which can ensure the good of all—God alone is everywhere and everything. We pray to Him and meditate on Him in the form of the effulgence of the sun. May He inspire us and guide us so that our intellect may remain steady on the right path. (Please also see para 2.2).

2.28. "Happiness of all" was to be recognized as the highest goal of life, for all the members of the society. Of course, Vedic hymns conveyed this message in Vedic Sanskrit. But a popular version thereof, expressed in classical Sanskrit (which is different from Vedic Sanskrit) will be presented in para 2.30. The opening words of the popular version, when translated into English, are "May all be happy".

2.29. अपामीवामप विश्वामनाहुतिं
अपारातिं दुर्विदत्रामघायतः ।
आरे देवा द्वेषो अस्मत्
युयोतनोरु णः शर्म यच्छता स्वस्तये ॥ ऋ० 10.63.12

apāmīvāmapa vishvāmanāhutim
apārātiṁ durvidatrāmaghāyataḥ
āre devā dveṣo asmat
yuyotanoru ṇaḥ sharma yacchatā svastaye
—*Rigveda* 10.63.12

Simple meaning—O God, make us free from diseases. Keep us firmly on the path of doing good to all. Keep us far away from those who do not help others. May we never cause conflict in the society. May all of us be happy and peaceful.

2.30. The preceding hymn summarizes the Vedic message of peace in Vedic Sanskrit. A popular version of that, expressed in classical Sanskrit, is now presented:

सर्वे भवन्तु सुखिनः सर्वे सन्तु निरामयाः ।
सर्वे भद्राणि पश्यन्तु मा कश्चिद् दुःखभाग् भवेत् ॥

sarve bhavantu sukhinaḥ
sarve santu nirāmayāḥ
sarve bhadrāṇi pashyantu
mā kashcid duhkhabhāg bhavet

Simple meaning—May all be happy, may all be free from diseases, may all look to the good of others, may none suffer from sorrow.

All Hindus recite this verse as a part of their prayer.

2.31. All the members of the society were to exemplify, among themselves, the practical application of the Vedic message of peace. That is, they were to establish freely chosen unity, and to contribute to public health awareness and moral strength of the society. All the four Vedas provided inspiration for such happiness-promoting efforts (although the hymns presented here are from two of them, viz. Rigveda and Atharvaveda).

2.32. समानी व आकूतिः
समाना हृदयानि वः ।
समानमस्तु वो मनो
यथा वः सु सहासति ॥ ऋ० 10.191.4

samānī va ākūtiḥ
samānā hridayāni vaḥ
samānamastu vo mano
yathā vaḥ su sahāsati —*Rigveda* 10.191.4

Simple meaning—Listen, O men and women, may you all think along similar lines, may you all cultivate feelings of heart-felt unity, may you all have similar aspirations. Only in this way can you make your society strong and prosperous.

2.33. उद्बुध्यध्वं समनसः सखायः
समग्निमिध्वं बहवः सनीलाः
दधिक्रामग्निमुषसं च
देवीमिन्द्रावतोऽवसे निह्वये वः ॥ ऋ० 10.101.1

udbudhyadhvaṁ samanasaḥ sakhāyaḥ
samagnimidhvaṁ bahavaḥ sanīlāḥ

dadhikrāmagnimuṣasaṁ ca
devīmindrāvatovase nihvaye vaḥ

—*Rigveda* 10.101.1

Simple meaning—Listen, O men and women, arise, awake, and be wise. Equip yourself with right thinking and right knowledge. Perform nicely your family activities, together. Move ahead with fortitude. May you receive full protection from divine and worldly powers.

2.34. कृषन्नित्फाल आशितं कृणोति
यन्नध्वानमप वृंक्ते चरित्रैः ।
वदन्ब्रह्माऽवदतो वनीयान्
पृणन्नापिरपृणन्तमभि स्यात् ॥ ऋ० 10.117.7

kriṣannitphāla āshitaṁ kriṇoti
yannadhvānamapa vrinkte caritraiḥ
vadanbrahmāvadato vanīyān
priṇannāpirapriṇantamabhi syāt

—*Rigveda* 10.117.7

Simple meaning—Listen, O men and women, be active and inspire others to be active too. Learn this lesson from the farmer, learn this lesson from the courier. Be not silent spectators in social life. Pass on your knowledge to others, and be not a miser while giving to the needy.

2.35. आकूतिं देवीं सुभगां पुरो दधे
चित्तस्य माता सुहवा नो अस्तु ।
यामाशामेमि केवली सा मे अस्तु
विदेयमेनां मनसि प्रविष्टाम् ॥ अ० 19.4.2

ākūtiṁ devīṁ subhagāṁ puro dadhe
cittasya mātā suhavā no astu
yāmāshāmemi kevalī sā me astu
videyamenāṁ manasi praviṣṭām

—*Atharvaveda* 19.4.2

Simple meaning—O God, we will give priority to right thinking, we will look upon this as your message. Right thinking will guide our actions, like our mother. Right thinking will determine the course of our life. Right thinking will constantly advise us, in the form of inner voice.

2.36. शतं जीवन्तु शरदः
पुरूचीरन्तर्मृत्युं दधतां पर्वतेन ॥ ऋ० 10.18.4

shataṁ jīvantu sharadaḥ
purūcīrantarmrityuṁ dadhatāṁ parvatena
—*Rigveda* 10.18.4

Simple meaning—Listen, O men and women, acquire strength like a mountain.Then death cannot overpower you, and you can stay healthy and active for hundred years.

2.37. All the members of the society were to cultivate open-mindedness and toleration, in the interest of maintaining peaceful social relationships. All the four Vedas provided guidance on this point (although the hymns presented here are from two of them, viz. Yajurveda and Atharvaveda).

2.38. सं वो मनांसि सं व्रता
समाकूतीर्नमामसि ।
अमी मे विव्रता स्थन
तान्वः सं नमयामसि ॥ अ० 6.94.1

saṁ vo manāṁsi saṁvratā
samākūtīrnamāmasi
amī me vivratā sthana
tānvaḥ saṁ namayāmasi —*Atharvaveda* 6.94.1

Simple meaning—Listen, O men and women, may you be able to bend, in the right direction, your mind, actions and thoughts. May you, in particular, be able to bend, in the right direction, your anti-social thoughts.

2.39. सुश्रुतिश्च मोपश्रुतिश्च
मा हासिष्टाम् ॥ अ० 16.2.5

sushrutishca mopashrutishca
mā hāsiṣṭām —*Atharvaveda* 16.2.5

Simple meaning—O God, give us the wisdom so that we may always listen to good advice. Also, give us the wisdom so that we may always accept the good advice.

2.40. मेधां सायं मेधां प्रात:
मेधां मध्यं दिनं परि ।
मेधां सूर्यस्य रश्मिभि:
वचसा वेशयामहे ॥ अ० 6.108.5

medhāṁ sāyaṁ medhāṁ prātaḥ
medhāṁ madhyaṁ dinaṁ pari
medhāṁ sūryasya rashmibhiḥ
vacasā veshayāmahe —*Atharvaveda* 6.108.5

Simple meaning—May we seek wisdom, day and night. May we absorb wisdom, like sun's rays, and may that wisdom be reflected from us in the form of wise words.

2.41. असंतापं मे हृदयमुर्वी गव्यूति: ।
समुद्रो अस्मि विधर्मणा ॥ अ० 16.3.6

asamṭāpaṁ me hridayamurvī gavyūtiḥ
samudro asmi vidharmaṇā —*Atharvaveda* 16.3.6

Simple meaning—May we be like ocean, accepting every thing that comes in, agreeable as well as disagreeable. May our mind and heart ever remain peaceful, irrespective of what we go through.

2.42. यां मेधां देवगणा:
पितरश्चोपासते ।
तया मामद्य मेधयाग्ने
मेधाविनं कुरु स्वाहा इदं न मम ॥ य० 32.14

yāṁ medhāṁ devagaṇāḥ
pitarashcopasate
tayā māmadya medhayāgne
medhāvinaṁ kuru svāhā idaṁ na mama
—*Yajurveda* 32.14

Simple meaning—I am seeking wisdom, which made my ancestors wise. May wisdom come to me today. For this, I offer whatever I have. In fact, whatever I have, is not mine, because it is God's.

The words 'idam na mama' (meaning 'it is not mine') are uttered at the end of each hymn while performing a yajna (a religious ceremony), the underlying idea being to declare one's gratefulness to God. Such an attitude promotes a sense of equality in society.

Vedic message of peace from the religious angle

2.43. Paras 2.3-2.42 have given a strong message of peace from the social angle. The following paras will show how this message is further strengthened by the Vedic ideas on religion. The presentation will be under five main points.

2.44. According to the Vedas, the universe is upheld by 'Sat' (*i.e.* Reality) which is One, which has no beginning and no end, which is formless and nameless. Words can never describe that Reality completely, but wise people can try to explain it to common people, not fully but partially, by making use of expressions like Indra, Agni, Varuṇa,etc. which correspond to rain, energy, orderliness, respectively. This approach of the Vedas has been wrongly interpreted as 'polytheism'. Rather, a useful message can be drawn from this, viz. that quarrelling over different names of God (and insisting on using only one particular name) cannot be justified.

2.45. एकं सद् विप्रा बहुधा वदन्ति ॥ ऋ० 1.164.46

ekaṁ sad viprā bahudhā vadanti

—*Rigveda* 1.164.46

Simple meaning—Reality is One, wise people call it by many names.

2.46. न द्वितीयो न तृतीयश्चतुर्थो नाप्युच्यते ।
न पंचमो न षष्ठः सप्तमो नाप्युच्यते ॥
नाष्टमो न नवमो दशमो नाप्युच्यते ॥ अ० 13.4.2

na dvitīyo na tritīyashcaturtho nāpyucyate
na pancamo na ṣaṣṭhah saptamo nāpyucyate
nāṣṭamo na navamo dashamo nāpyucyate

—*Atharvaveda* 13.4.2

Simple meaning—Reality is One. There is no second Reality, nor third, nor fourth. Similarly, there is no fifth Reality, nor sixth, nor seventh. Again, there is no eighth Reality, nor ninth, nor tenth.

2.47. न तस्य प्रतिमा अस्ति
यस्य नाम महद् यशः ॥ य० 32.3

na tasya pratimā asti
yasya nāma mahad yashaḥ —*Yajurveda* 32.3

Simple meaning—Reality is formless and nameless. Reality is Infinite. Wise people give it a name for purposes of singing its glories.

2.48. यत्र विश्वं भवत्येकनीडम् ।
तस्मिन्निदं संच वि चैति सर्वं ॥
स ओतः प्रोतश्च विभूः प्रजासु ॥ य० 32.8

yatra vishvaṁ bhavatyekanīdam
tasminnidaṁ sanca vi caiti sarvam
sa otaḥ protashca vibhūḥ prajāsu

—*Yajurveda* 32.8

Simple meaning—Reality is One,the entire universe is embedded in it. Whatever we see, comes out of that Reality, and goes back into it. Human beings too come out of that Reality, and go back into it.

2.49. त्वं स्त्री त्वं पुमानसि ।
त्वं कुमार उत वा कुमारी ॥
त्वं जीर्णो दण्डेन वंचसि ॥ अ० 10.8.27

tvaṁ strī tvaṁ pumānasi
tvaṁ kumāra uta vā kumārī
tvaṁ jīrṇo danḍena vancasi

—*Atharvaveda* 10.8.27

Simple meaning—O God, you take the form of a woman, you take the form of a man. You take the form of a boy, you take the form of a girl. You take the form of old people who walk with the help of a stick.

2.50. इन्द्रं मित्रं वरुणमग्निमाहुरथो ॥ ऋ० 1.164.46

indraṁ mitraṁ varuṇamagnimāhuratho
—*Rigveda* 1.164.46

Simple meaning—Indra, Mitra, Varuna, Agni—these are some of the names given to Reality.

2.51. Reality is humanity's mother and father, protector, giver of prosperity, giver of the message of fearlessness, and also the message of concern for one another. The underlying message is that God wants all the people to care for one another.

2.52. त्वं हि नः पिता वसो त्वं माता
शतक्रतो बभूविथ ॥ ऋ० 8.98.11

tvaṁ hi naḥ pitā vaso tvaṁ mātā
shatakrato babhūvitha —*Rigveda* 8.98.11

Simple meaning—O God, you are our father, you are our mother. You are the shelter for all, and because of you, we are able to live and do good deeds.

2.53. महीरस्य प्रणीतयः ।
पूर्वीरुत प्रशस्तयः ।
नास्य क्षीयन्त ऊतयः ॥ ऋ० 6.45.3

mahīrasya praṇītayaḥ
pūrvīruta prashastayaḥ
nāsya kṣīyanta ūtayaḥ —*Rigveda* 6.45.3

Simple meaning—God's glories are endless. He has been protecting the world and will keep on doing the same for ever. Prayers to God can be offered in many ways.

2.54. त्वं विश्वस्य धनदा असि ।
तवायं विश्वः पुरुहूत पार्थिवः
अवस्युर्नाम भिक्षते ॥ ऋ० 7.32.17

twaṁ vishvasya dhanadā asi
tavāyaṁ vishvaḥ puruhūta pārthivaḥ
avasyurnāma bhikṣate —*Rigveda* 7.32.17

Simple meaning—O God, you are the giver of prosperity to the whole world. All mankind prays to you and seeks your blessings so that their life and prosperity may remain protected.

2.55. उताभये पुरुहूत श्रवोभिरेको
दृढमवदो वृत्रहा सन् ।
इमे चिदिन्द्र रोदसी अपारे
यत्संगृभ्णा मघवन् काशिरित्ते ॥ ऋ० 3.30.5

utābhaye puruhūta shravobhireko
driḍhamavado vritrahā san
ime cidindra rodasī apāre
yatsangribhṇā maghavan kāshiritte
—*Rigveda* 3.30.5

Simple meaning—O God, you have made us fearless. Through inspiring mantras (hymns), Vedas have given us assurance: "Be not afraid of any evil force because God always overpowers evil." You are upholding all these worlds—they need not fear because they are under your protection.

This hymn clarifies the Vedic approach that God is the only power in the universe (there is no Satan or Devil). Furthermore, the use of the Vedic expression: "Sangribhna" in this hymn is significant because it facilitated the formulation, in classical Sanskrit, of the Bhagavad-Gita's concept of "Lokasamgraha" (meaning: good of the world or good of all). (Please see para 4.26).

2.56. भद्रं वै वरं वृणते
भद्रं युञ्जन्ति दक्षिणम् ।
भद्रं वैवस्वते चक्षुः
बहुत्रा जीवतो मनः ॥ ऋ० 10.164.2

bhadraṁ vai varaṁ vriṇate
bhadraṁ yunjanti dakṣiṇam
bhadraṁ vaivasvate cakṣuḥ
bahutrā jīvato manaḥ —*Rigveda* 10.164.2

Simple meaning—O God, you have taught us that, to do good to others is the best thought. You have also taught us that this should be done skilfully, to the best of one's capability. Furthermore, you have taught us: "See no evil, hear no evil, speak no evil, think no evil".

2.57. When we pray to God, the best thing that we can ask for is 'right thinking and right intellect'- this being the religious message of Gayatri Mantra. The social message of Gayatri Mantra (along with the mantra itself) has been given in para 2.27. So it is not necessary to write here, the Gayatri Mantra again. But we would like to illustrate as to what a Gayatri Mantra based prayer could be, by quoting from Rabindra Nath Tagore's "Gitanjali"-

> This is my prayer to thee, my lord,
> Strike, strike at the root of penury in my heart.
> Give me the strength lightly to bear my joys and sorrows.
> Give me the strength to make my love fruitful in service
> Give me the strength never to disown the poor or bend my knees before insolent might
> Give me the strength to raise my mind high above daily trifles
> And give me the strength to surrender my strength to thy will with love.[1]

2.58. Open-mindedness in religious matters is a great virtue-this message has been given in the Vedas in various contexts. The most popular section of the Vedas, from which this message has been drawn, is called "nasadiya sukta" or the Vedic hymn of creation. As to the creation of the universe, the Vedas declared that no one can ever give a definitive answer. The upanisadic expression "neti"(meaning, not this, also meaning, not the end) summarizes that Vedic declaration. In order to convey the details,we reproduce here the Vedic hymn of creation, from the Rigveda.

2.59. नासदासीन्नो सदासीत्तदानीं
नासीद्रजो नो व्योमा परो यत् ।
किमावरीवः कुह कस्य शर्मन्
अम्भः किमासीद् गहनं गभीरम् ॥ ऋ० 10.129.1

nāsadāsīnno sadāsīttadānīm
nāsīdrajo no vyomā paro yat
kimāvarīvaḥ kuha kasya sharman
ambhaḥ kimāsīd gahanaṁ gabhīram
—*Rigveda* 10.129.1

Simple meaning—We follow the advice of S. Radhakrishnan and C.A. Moore,[2] and give below the meaning of this hymn in the poetic language of A. A. Macdonell—

Non-being then existed not, nor being:
There was no air, nor sky that is beyond it.
What was concealed? Wherein? In whose protection?
And was there deep unfathomable water?

2.60. न मृत्युरासीदमृतं न तर्हि
न रात्र्या अह्न आसीत् प्रकेतः।
आनीदवातं स्वधया तदेकं
तस्माद् हान्यन्न पुरः किं चनास ॥ ऋ ० 10.129.2

na mrityurāsīdamritaṁ na tarhi
na rātryā ahna āsīt praketaḥ
ānīdavātaṁ svadhayā tadekaṁ
tasmād hānyanna puraḥ kiṁ canāsa
—*Rigveda* 10.129.2

Simple meaning—(Macdonell's version)—
Death then existed not, nor life immortal;
Of neither night nor day was any token .
By its inherent force the One breathed windless;
No other thing than that beyond existed.

2.61. तम आसीत्तमसा गूलहमग्रे
अप्रकेतं सलिलं सर्वमा इदम् ।
तुच्छ्येनाभ्वपिहितं यदासीत्

तपसस्तन्महिना जायतैकम् ॥ ऋ० 10.129.3

tama āsīttamasā gūlahamagre
apraketaṁ salilaṁ sarvamā idam
tucchyenābhvapihitaṁ yadāsīt
tapasastanmahinā jāyataikam

—*Rigveda* 10.129.3

Simple meaning—(Macdonell's version)—

Darkness there was at first by darkness hidden;
Without distinctive marks, this all was water.
That which, becoming, by the void was covered,
That one by force of heat came into being.

2.62. कामस्तदग्रे समवर्तताधि
मनसो रेतः प्रथमं यदासीत् ।
सतो बन्धुमसति निरविन्दन्
हृदि प्रतीष्या कवयो मनीषा ॥ ऋ० 10.129.4

kāmastadagre samavartatādhi
manaso retaḥ prathamaṁ yadāsīt
sato bandhumasati niravindan
hridi pratīṣyā kavayo manīṣā —*Rigveda* 10.129.4

Simple meaning—(Macdonell's version)—

Desire entered the One in the beginning:
It was the earliest seed, of thought the product.
The sages searching in their hearts with wisdom,
Found out the bond of being in non-being.

2.63. तिरश्चीनो विततो रश्मिरेषां
अधः स्विदासीदुपरि स्विदासीत् ।
रेतोधा आसन्महिमान आसन्
स्वधा अवस्तात्प्रयतिः परस्तात् ॥ ऋ० 10.129.5

tirashcīno vitato rashmireṣām
adhaḥ svidāsīdupari svidāsīt
retodhā āsanmahimāna āsan
svadhā avastātprayatiḥ parastāt

—*Rigveda* 10.129.5

Simple meaning—(Macdonell's version)—

Their ray extended light across the darkness:
But was the One above or was it under?
Creative force was there, and fertile power:
Below was energy, above was impulse.

2.64. को अद्धा वेद क इह प्र वोचत्
कुत आजाता कुत इयं विसृष्टि : ।
अर्वाग्देवा अस्य विसर्जनेन
अथा को वेद यत आ बभूव ॥ ऋ० 10.129.6

ko addhā veda ka iha pra vocat
kuta ājātā kuta iyaṁ visriṣṭih
arvāgdevā asya visarjanena
athā ko veda yata ā babhūva

—*Rigveda* 10.129.6

Simple meaning—(Macdonell's version)—

Who knows for certain? Who shall here declare it?
Whence was it born, and whence came this creation
The gods were born after this world's creation:
Then who can know from whence it has arisen?

2.65. इयं विसृष्टिर्यत आ बभूव
यदि वा दधे यदि वा न ।
यो अस्याध्यक्ष : परमे व्योमन्
सो अंग वेद यदि वा न वेद ॥ ऋ० 10.129.7

iyaṁ visriṣṭiryata ā babhūva
yadi vā dadhe yadi vā na
yo asyādhyaksaḥ parame vyoman
so anga veda yadi vā na veda

—*Rigveda* 10.129.7

Simple meaning—(Macdonell's version)—

None knoweth whence creation has arisen;
And whether he has or has not produced it;
He who surveys it in the highest heaven,
He only knows, or haply he may know not.

2.66. Peace between human beings can be facilitated if it is viewed as a part of 'all round peace' which includes peace between human beings and nature, as well as peace between human beings and God (which means viewing God as the maker of peace, i.e.well-wisher of all human beings, irrespective of their religious beliefs). This is the religious message which needs to be derived from Shanti-patha (or Vedic hymn of all-round peace), a part of which was presented in para 2.10. The full text of Shanti-patha is given below—

पृथिवी शान्तिरन्तरिक्षं शान्तिर्द्यौः
शान्तिराप : शान्तिरोषधय: शान्तिर्वनस्पतय:
शान्तिर्विश्वे देवाः शान्तिः सर्वे देवाः
शान्तिः शान्तिः शान्तिः शान्तिभिः शान्तिः ।
ताभिः शान्तिभिः सर्वशान्तिभिः शमया मोहं ॥
यदिह घोरं यदिह क्रूरं यदिह पापं
तच्छान्तं तच्छिवं सर्वमेव शमस्तु नः ॥

–अ० 19.9.14

prithivī shāntirantariksaṁ shāntirdyauḥ
shāntirāpaḥ shāntiroṣadhayaḥ shāntirvanaspatayaḥ
shāntirvishve devāḥ shāntiḥ sarve devāḥ
shāntiḥ shāntiḥ shāntiḥ shāntibhiḥ shāntiḥ
tābhiḥ shāntibhiḥ sarvashāntibhiḥ shamayā moham
yadiha ghoraṁ yadiha krūraṁ yadiha pāpam
tacchāntaṁ tacchivaṁ sarvameva shamastu naḥ

—*Atharvaveda* 19.9.14

Simple meaning—May mother earth give us peace, may the sky give us peace, may all the worlds give us peace, may the oceans give us peace, may all the plants give us peace, may all vegetation give us peace, may mother nature give us peace, may all divine powers give us peace. May there be all-round peace. May there be peace in all directions. May all human beings experience peace and be free from ignorance.

Whatever is harsh, may that become peaceful
Whatever is cruel, may that become kind

Whatever is unrighteous, may that become purified
May all achieve peace. May none be put to harm.

Applications

2.67. The advice of the Vedas that peace promotion should be a two-pronged process, viz. social as well as religious, has been repeated in the Bhagavad-Gita as well as in the Mahabharata, and has, in modern times, been accepted by peace-activists in general. For example, Swami Vivekananda coined, in 1897,[3] the following phrase (in Sanskrit) for purposes of providing the motto to Ramakrishna Mission:

आत्मनो मोक्षार्थं जगद्धिताय च

ātmano moksārthaṁ jagaddhitāya ca

Simple meaning—For one's spiritual liberation as well as for the good of the world.

2.68. On the social front, the Vedic message (as expressed in classical Sanskrit- reference para 2.30), and particularly its abridged form, viz.

सर्वे भवन्तु सुखिनः

sarve bhavantu sukhinaḥ

Simple meaning—May all be happy—has been widely recognized as having the biggest potential for establishing social harmony. The Bhagavad-Gita coined a shorter expression: "Lokasamgraha" to convey the same message (Please see para 4.26).

2.69. On the religious front, the Vedic appeal for open-mindedness (reference para 2.58) has been conveyed in beautiful English by Rabindranath Tagore, for the benefit of the modern society:

Where the mind is without fear and the head is held high;
Where knowledge is free;
Where the world has not been broken up into fragments by narrow domestic walls;

Where words come out from the depth of truth;
Where tireless striving stretches its arms towards perfection;
Where the clear stream of reason has not lost its way into the dreary desert sand of dead habit;
Where the mind is led forward by thee into ever-widening thought and action-
Into that heaven of freedom, my Father, let my country awake.[4]

CHAPTER 3

The Upanisadic Philosophy of Oneness of All Human Beings

3.1. The Vedas gave a socio-religious message of peace, as described in the preceding chapter. The Upanisads strengthened this message by providing the philosophical support thereto. In plain language, while the Vedas advised people to help one another and to harm no one, the Upanisads said, "You and others are all one, therefore if you harm any one, you are harming yourself." This type of support from the Upanisads can be viewed as a natural consequence of the fact that the Upanisads are really a part of the Vedas themselves, and that they repeat some of the Vedic hymns. For example, Svetasvatara Upanisad contains the following hymn which originally occurs in Atharvaveda (reference para 2.49)—

त्वं स्त्री त्वं पुमानसि ।
त्वं कुमार उत वा कुमारी ॥
त्वं जीर्णो दण्डेन वञ्चसि ॥ श्वेताश्वतर उप० 4.3

tvaṁ strī tvaṁ pumānasi
tvaṁ kumāra uta vā kumārī
tvaṁ jīrṇo daṇḍena vancasi

—*Svetasvatara Up.* 4.3

Simple meaning—O God, you take the form of a woman, you take the form of a man. You take the form of a boy, you take the form of a girl. You take the form of old people who walk with the help of a stick.

3.2. The unifying philosophy of the Upanisads is called 'monism' which is different from monotheism in a number of ways, as briefly explained below:-

(a) In monism, the Ultimate Reality is One, Impersonal (i.e. formless), and Unknowable. Upanisads call 'It' Brahman (which is neither male nor female, and therefore can not be referred to as 'He'). The universe came out of that Reality (i.e. Brahman), and all that we see has come out of Brahman and will go back to Brahman. (To talk of heaven and hell is inconsistent with this). All human beings are essentially one, although they appear to be different. The differences between human beings have arisen due to their Karma (i.e. actions). Mutual relationships between human beings should be guided more by their oneness, rather than by their differences. To put an end to conflicts, an appeal should be made to the divine element in every human being (called Atman). Radhakrishnan and Moore have pointed out that the correct word for Atman in English is self, not soul.[1] About the Oneness of Brahman, and the identity of Brahman and Atman, Mandukya Upanisad says:

सर्वं हि एतद् ब्रह्म ।
अयमात्मा ब्रह्म ॥ मांडूक्य उप० 1.2

sarvaṁ hi etad brahma
ayamātmā brahma —*Mandukya Up.* 1.2

Simple meaning—Everything here is Brahman. The Atman of every human being is Brahman.

Finally, it should be added that, according to Upanisads, there is no Satan (the Devil).

(b) In monotheism, the creator of the universe is One, personal God. He created all the human beings. But Satan (the Devil) tries to mislead people into doing anti-social acts. God protects.

3.3. Although the total number of Upanisads is usually mentioned as 108, those readily available in print are 18. All of them present the philosophy of oneness of all human beings, from different angles. The simplest imagery used by modern scholars to convey the basic message of this philosophy is in terms of the relationship between the ocean and the water-drops, on the one hand, and the Universal Self and individual selves, on the other. Traditionally, the emphasis has been on the four mahavakyas[2] (i.e. Great statements of the Upanisads). We feel, however, that, for our present purpose, it is not necessary to go into details of metaphysics (because that could make this chapter too long). Therefore, we have presented only one of the four mahavakyas (viz. the second part of the quotation from Mandukya Upanisad given in the preceding para). In the next para, we shall make a brief reference to the Upanisadic approach to creation, but thereafter we shall devote the rest of the chapter to applications of the Upansadic philosophy to world peace. Here it should be mentioned that the Upanisadic philosophy is called 'Vedanta'.

3.4. We want to refer briefly to the Upanisadic approach to creation (which broadly supports evolution) because Sri Aurobindo has expanded it to include therein his own theory of Spiritual Evolution (which has implications for world peace). Our purpose will be served by presenting here the following extract from Chandogya Upanisad:

तद्ध एके आहुः । असदेवेदमग्रे आसीत् एकमेवाद्वितीयम् ।
तस्मात् असतः सत् जायत ।
कुतस्तु खलु सोम्य एवं स्यादिति होवाच । कथमसतः
सत् जायेतेति । सत्त्वेव सोम्य इदमग्रे आसीत्
एकमेवाद्वितीयम् ।
तदैक्षत । बहु स्यां प्रजायेयेति । तत् तेजोऽसृजत ।
तत्तेज ऐक्षत । बहुस्यां प्रजायेयेति । तद् अपोऽसृजत ।
ता आप ऐक्षंत । बह्व्यः स्याम प्रजायेमहीति ।
ता अन्नमसृजन्त ॥ छान्दोग्य उप० 6.2. 1-4.

taddha eke āhuḥ. asadevedamagre āsīt ekamevādvitīyam. tasmāt asataḥ sat jāyata. kutastu khalu somya evaṁ syāditi hovāca kathamasatah sat jāyeteti. Sattveva somya

idamagre āsīt ekamevādvitīyam.
tadaiksata. bahu syāṁ prajāyeyeti. tat tejosrijata.
tatteja aiksata. bahu syām prajāyeyeti. tat aposrijata
tā āpa aiksanta bahvyah syāma prajāyemahīti.
tā annamasrijanta —*Chandogya Up.* 6.2.1-4

Simple meaning—Aruni spoke to his son Svetaketu, "My dear, I will tell you about creation. But first, listen to what some people say: 'In the beginning, this world was just Non-being (asat), one only, without a second; from that Non-being, Being (Sat) was produced'. "But, my dear, how could this possibly happen? How from Non-being, could Being be produced?" "Now, my dear, I will tell you about creation. In the beginning, this world was just Being, one only, without a second. It bethought itself: 'Would that I were many! Let me procreate myself!' Thus, energy (tejas) was produced. Then, energy bethought itself: 'Would that I were many! Let me procreate myself!' Thus, water was produced. Then, water bethought itself: 'Would that I were many! Let me procreate myself!' Thus, food was produced."

Applications to World Peace

3.5. The Upanisads have inspired countless people, for thousands of years, to promote social harmony. Their contribution is particularly significant because their message is universal (non-denominational). Since problems of world peace have been aggravated in modern times, it will be more appropriate to focus attention on recent events—and this will be more convincing because of the availability of recorded information. Specifically, we take the year 1893 as the starting point for this purpose, because the Parliament of World Religions was held in that year, in Chicago (USA), and Swami Vivekananda viewed that conference as making a significant contribution to inter-religious harmony and peace. This means that inter-religious conflicts that we see today, would have been even worse if that conference had not taken place. At that conference, Swami Vivekananda, quoting from the Upanisads, delivered a strong message of hope and continuation of collaborative effort, in the cause of peace-and it is known that his message was recognized as the high-point of the conference. We present this as the first major application of Upanisadic ideas, in modern times, to uphold and maintain the spirit of universal dedication to harmony and peace. (This will be followed by ten more applications).

Appeal to peace-loving people not to lose heart

3.6. Here is an extract from Swami Vivekananda's address to the Parliament of World Religions, 1893, in the course of which he quoted from Katha Upanisad:

"Sectarianism, bigotry, and its horrible descendant, fanaticism, have long possessed this beautiful earth.... They have filled the earth with violence, drenched it often and often with human blood, destroyed civilization and sent whole nations to despair.... But their time has come, and I fervently hope that the bell that tolled this morning in honor of this convention may be the death-knell of all fanaticism... because at the head of this universe, in and through every particle of matter and force, stands One 'by whose command the wind blows, the fire burns, the clouds rain, the sun shines, and death too carries out its allotted task.' "[3]

The hymn from Katha Upanisad (the simple meaning of which is given above within quotation marks) is presented below:

भयादस्याग्निस्तपति भयात्तपति सूर्यः ।
भयादिन्द्रश्च वायुश्च मृत्युर्धावति पंचमः ॥

–कठ उप० 6.3

bhayādasyāgnistapati bhayāttapati sūryaḥ
bhayādindraśca vāyuśca mrityurdhāvati pancamaḥ

—*Katha Up.* 6.3

(The simple meaning of this hymn is contained in Swami Vivekananda's address).

Tagore's poem that spread the Upanisadic message world-wide

3.7. Rabindra Nath Tagore[4] (who received the Nobel Prize for Literature in 1913) travelled to many countries and spread the Upanisadic message of oneness of all human beings. One of the most popular of Tagore's poems, titled 'Old and New' became famous for conveying the message: 'Alien there is none', and this was translated into several European languages too. We present it as application # 2.

" Thou hast made me known to friends whom I knew not
Thou hast given me seats in homes not my own.
Thou hast brought the distant near,
And made me a brother of the stranger.

" I am uneasy at heart
When I have to leave my accustomed shelter,
I forget that there abides the old and the new,
And that there also thou abidest.

" Through birth and death, in this world or in others,
Wherever thou leadest me it is thou, the same,
The One companion of my endless life
Who ever linkest my heart
With bonds of joy to the Unfamiliar.

"When one knows thee, then alien there is none,
Then no door is shut.
Oh, grant me my prayer that I may never lose
The bliss of the touch of the one
In the play of the many."

Inter-religious collaboration for peace

3.8. The Vedas had given the message (reference para 2.44) that quarrelling over different names of God cannot be justified, because:

एकं सद् विप्रा बहुधा वदन्ति ॥ ऋ० 1.164.46

ekaṁ sad viprā bahudhā vadanti

Simple meaning—Reality is One,wise people call it by many names.

The Upanisads broadened this message by saying that quarrelling over different books (of religion) cannot be justified, because:

ग्रन्थमभ्यस्य मेधावी
ज्ञानविज्ञानतत्त्वतः ।
पलालमिव धान्यार्थी
त्यजेद् ग्रन्थं अशेषतः ॥ ब्रह्मबिन्दु उप० 1.7

granthamabhyasya medhāvī
jnānavijnānatattvātaḥ
palālamiva dhānyarthī
tyajed granthaṁ asheṣataḥ —*Brahmabindu Up.*1.7

Simple meaning—Wise people, after extracting the essence of a book, need not cling to the book itself, just as farmers, after obtaining the grain from the husk, need not cling to the husk.

Referring to these messages, which can help inter-religious collaboration for peace,Will Durant wrote in 1935:

"India will teach us the tolerance and gentleness of the mature mind, the quiet content of the unacquisitive soul, the calm of the understanding spirit, and a unifying, pacifying love for all living things."[5]

The outstanding contribution of Ram Krishna Paramahansa (Guru of Swami Vivekananda) in this field was acknowledged by Kazi Nazrul Islam,[6] a well-known Muslim poet of Bengal, in the following words of recognition (written in memory of Ram Krishna Paramhansa):

मंदिरे मस्जिदे गिर्जाय
पूजिले ब्रह्मे समश्रद्धाय ।
तव नाम माखा प्रेम निकेतने
भरियाचे ताइ त्रिसंसार ॥

mandire masjide girjāy
pūjīle brahme samashraddhāy
tava nām mākhā prem niketane
bhariyāche tāi trisamsār

Simple meaning—Thou didst worship God with equal fervour in temple, mosque, and church, for which reason the whole world is filled with the reservoir of Love that Thou art.

Message of tolerance, sharing and compassion

3.9. A strong message of tolerance, sharing and compassion has been given by the Upanisads, directly too. For example, the following story from Brihadaranyak Upanisad highlights three words (two of which obviously mean sharing and compassion, respectively, and the third one has several meanings (given in the Mahabharata) which include tolerance also:

त्रया: प्राजापत्या: । प्रजापतौ पितरि ब्रह्मचर्यमूषु: ।
देवा मनुष्या असुरा: । उषित्वा ब्रह्मचर्यं । देवा ऊचु: ।
ब्रवीतु नो भवानिति । तेभ्यो ह एतदक्षरमुवाच द इति ।
व्यज्ञासिष्टा इति । व्यज्ञासिष्मेति होचु: । दाम्यतेति
न आत्थेति । ओमिति होवाच व्यज्ञासिष्टेति ॥

अथ हैनं मनुष्या ऊचु: । ब्रवीतु नो भवानिति । तेभ्यो
ह एतदेवाक्षरमुवाच द इति । व्यज्ञासिष्टा इति ।
व्यज्ञासिष्मेति होचु: । दत्तेति न आत्थेति ।
ओमिति होवाच व्यज्ञासिष्टेति ॥

अथ हैनं असुरा ऊचु: । ब्रवीतु नो भवानिति । तेभ्यो
ह एतदेवाक्षरमुवाच द इति । व्यज्ञासिष्टा इति ।
व्यज्ञासिष्मेति होचु: । दयध्वमिति न आत्थेति । ओमिति
होवाच व्यज्ञासिष्टेति । तदेतदेव एषा दैवी वाक्
अनुवदति स्तनयित्नु: द द द इति । दाम्यत दत्त
दयध्वमिति । तदेतत् त्रयं शिक्षेत् । दमं दानं दयामिति ॥

–बृहदारण्यक उप० 5.2.1-3

tyayāḥ prājāpatyāḥ prajāpatau pitari brahma-
charyamūṣuḥ. devā manuṣyā asurāḥ. uṣitvā

brahmacharyam. devā ūchuḥ .bravītu no bhavāniti tebhyo ha etadaksaramuvāca da iti . vyajnāsiṣṭā iti. vyajnāsiṣmeti hochuḥ . dāmyateti na āttheti. omiti hovacha vyajnāsiṣteti

atha hainaṁ manuṣyā ūchuḥ. bravītu no bhavāniti. tebhyo ha etadevāksaramuvācha da iti. vyajnāsiṣṭā iti. vyajnāsiṣmeti hochuḥ. datteti na āttheti. omiti hovācha vyajnāsiṣteti

atha hainaṁ asurā ūchuḥ. bravītu no bhavāniti. tebhyo ha etadevāksaramuvācha da iti vyajnāsistā iti. vyajnasismeṭi hochuḥ. dayadhvamiti na āttheti. Omiti hovācha vyajnāsiṣteti. tadetadeva eṣā daivī vāk anuvadati stanayitnuḥ da da da iti. dāmyata datta dayadhvamiti tadetat trayaṁ shikset. damam dānam dayāmiti —*brihadāraṇyak up.* 5.2.1-3

Simple meaning—Three categories of Prajapati's sons—gods, men, and demons—lived with their father as students. After finishing their studies, the gods said to Prajapati, "Please summarize to us your teaching." He told them the syllable 'da' and asked, "Have you understood?" The gods said , "We have. You say to us, discipline yourselves and cultivate tolerance." Prajapati said, "Yes, you have understood."

Then men said to him, "Please summarize to us your teaching." Prajapati told them the same syllable 'da' and asked, "Have you understood?" Men said , "We have. You say to us, share with others whatever you have." Prajapati said, "Yes. You have understood."

Then demons said to Prajapati, "Please summarize to us your teaching." Prajapati told them the same syllable 'da' and asked, "Have you understood ?" Demons said, "We have. You say to us, have compassion." Prajapati said, "Yes, you have understood."

The same thing does the divine voice, thunder, repeat: da , da, da, that is, cultivate tolerance, share with others whatever you have, have compassion. One should practice this same triad: tolerance, sharing, compassion. (The Sanskrit word for each of the three, starts with 'da').

Let eveyone obtain unifying education, and avoid fragmentation

3.10. The preceding para is illustrative of the fact that the Upanisads stress the importance of right education, viz. education that unites people and avoids fragmentation. Katha Upanisad gives the clarion call:

उत्तिष्ठत जाग्रत प्राप्य वरान्निबोधत ।

–कठ उप० 3.14

uttiṣṭhata jāgrata prāpya varānnibodhata

—*Kaṭha Up.* 3.14

Simple meaning—Arise, awake, find a good teacher, and obtain the right education.

Mundaka Upanisad advises that education should be broad-based:

द्वे विद्ये वेदितव्ये । परा चैवापरा च ।

–मुंडक उप० 1.1.2

dve vidye veditavye
parā chaivāparā cha. —*muṇḍaka Up.* 1.1.2

Simple meaning—Education should be complete and comprehensive. It should include knowledge of the world as well as knowledge of the Self.

Isha Upanisad clarifies the purpose of both types of education. But there is a difference in terminology. While referring to 'knowledge of the world,' Mundaka Upanisad uses the expression 'apara vidya'. The corresponding expression in Isha Upanisad is 'avidya'. Similarly, while referring to 'knowledge of the Self', Mundaka Upanisad uses the expression 'para vidya'. The corresponding expression in Isha Upanisad is 'vidya'. Now, the following hymn of Isha Upanisad:

विद्यां चाविद्यां च
यस्तद् वेदोभयं सह ।
अविद्यया मृत्युं तीर्त्वा
विद्ययामृतमश्नुते ॥ ईशा उप० 1.11

vidyāṁ chāvidyāṁ cha
yastad vedobhayaṁ saha
avidyayā mrityuṁ tīrtvā
vidyayāmritamashnute —*Isha Up.* 1.11

Simple meaning—While acquiring both types of knowledge, the unifying vision must be given the highest importance. For example, while acquiring 'knowledge of the world', the destructive elements (viz. division and fragmentation of society) must be avoided. Similarly, while acquiring 'knowledge of the Self', the life-saving elements (viz. unifying vision in theory as well as in practice) must be integrated with your personality.

A practical application of the above-mentioned Upanisadic message was attempted by Rabindra Nath Tagore when he started the educational institution: "Shanti Niketan" in Bengal (which later on became a University). The name of the institution is significant—it means 'abode of peace'. Along with the usual curriculum, the students also learnt there about the languages, cultures and religions of the neighbouring societies and this was done with a unifying vision (*i.e.* not to create ill will, but friendliness). During the course of his Nobel Prize Acceptance Speech, delivered at Stockholm in 1921, Tagore referred to the inspiration that he got from the Upanisads:

"We have inherited the immortal works of our ancestors, those great writers of Upanisads, who proclaimed the religion of unity and sympathy... I invite you to come to us and join hands with us and not to leave this institution merely to us, but let your own students and learned men come to us and help us to make this university a common institution for the East and the West. May they give the contributions of their lives and may we all together make it living and representative of the undivided Humanity of the world. For this I have come to you.

I ask you this and I claim it of you in the name of the unity of men, and in the name of love, and in the name of God. I ask you to come. I invite you."[7]

Let girls have equal opportunities for education

3.11. Although this point can broadly be covered by the preceding message that fragmentation in the field of education must be avoided, still the question of girls' education is so important, that it is better to draw particular attention to it. According to Upanisads, girls and boys have the same atman (self), therefore there is no justification for giving a low priority to girls' education. Svetasvatar Upanisad stated explicitly: (reference para 3.1):

त्वं कुमार उत वा कुमारी । श्वेताश्वतर उप० 4.3

tvam kumāra uta vā kumārī

—*Svetasvatar Up.* 4.3

Simple meaning—O God, you take the form of a boy, you take the form of a girl.

Chandogya Upanisad contains an assertion made by King Asvapati that in his kingdom, no one was uneducated i.e. that girls' education received the same attention as boys' education:

न मे स्तेनो जनपदे
न कदर्यो न मद्यपः ।
नानाहिताग्निर्नाविद्वान्
न स्वैरी स्वैरिणी कुतः ॥ छान्दोग्य उप० 5.11.5

na me steno janapade
na kadaryo na madyapaḥ
nānāhitāgnirnāvidvān
na svairī svairiṇī kutaḥ

—*Chandogya up.* 5.11.5

Simple meaning—King Asvapati told the visiting scholars, in my kingdom, there is no thief, no miser, no drunkard, no one deprived of fire, no uneducated, and no instance of adulterous affair between men and women.

In India, not only Tagore but all educationists have attached the highest importance to girls' education, i.e. they have fully accepted the advice of the Upanisads.

Oppose discrimination on any ground, but non-violently

3.12. The preceding paras presented the message of the Upanisads as 'unify the society on the basis of equality of all'. But what to do if some government or group of people disregards this message and follows a policy of discrimination on some ground or the other, say, race, color, creed, sex, age, etc. A reply to this question, based on the Upanisads, can be prepared, by combining the following four messages:

एष आत्मेति होवाच । एतदमृतमभयमेतद् ब्रह्मेति ।
तस्य ह वा एतस्य ब्रह्मणो नाम सत्यमिति ॥ –छांदोग्य उप० 8.3.4

eṣa ātmeti hovācha. etadamritamabhayametad
brahmeti. tasya ha vā etasya brahmaṇo
nāma satyamiti —*Chandogya Up.* 8.3.4

Simple meaning—The teacher said, I will tell you about Atman. It is deathless and fearless. It is the same as Brahman (the Ultimate Reality). It is truth.

सत्यमेव जयते नानृतम् । मुंउक उप० 3.1.6

satyameva jayate nānritam

—*mundaka up.* 3.1.6

Simple meaning—Truth alone wins. Untruth never wins.

नायमात्मा बलहीनेन लभ्यः । मुंडक उप० 3.2.4

nāyamātmā balahīnena labhyaḥ

—*mundaka up.* 3.2.4

Simple meaning—Atma (truth) can not be obtained by any one who does not have moral strength.

अहिंसां सत्यं च यत्नेन रक्षत । आरुणिक उप० 1.1

ahimsāṁ satyaṁ cha yatnena rakṣata

—*Arunika Up.* 1.1

Simple meaning—Non-violence and truth go together. Determined effort is needed to stick to them.

In order to apply a combination of the above-mentioned four Upanisadic messages, in the present context, we have composed the following verse:

> एकत्वं सर्वभूतेषु घर्मजातिभेदाद्विना ।
> भेदभावमुक्तये तु कर्तव्योऽहिंसको यत्नः ॥
>
> *ekatvaṁ sarvabhuteṣu*
> *dharmajātibhedādvinā*
> *bhedabhāvamuktaye tu*
> *kartavyohiṁsako yatnaḥ*

Simple meaning—Discrimination on any ground has to be opposed because it is a violation of the Upanisadic philosophy of oneness of all human beings. However, such opposition must be non-violent, and determined effort is needed to do that.

As a successful application of the above message, we want to mention Mahatma Gandhi's anti-discrimination struggle against the Government of South Africa, conducted during the years 1906-1914. Since it was the first struggle of this type in recorded history, Gandhi gave it a specific name : Satyagraha, which literally means: force of truth. Looking at it a century later, it seems worth pointing out that the starting date of this Satyagraha was 11th September 1906. We cannot possibly give here the details as to how success was achieved after eight years of determined effort. However, we present a short extract from R. Iyer's book on the subject:

"In the opinion of the historian P. Spratt, the Satyagraha in South Africa could be called a 'model', not only because it was the first use of the new technique but also because it stayed very close to the 'principles'. It was conducted against very heavy odds by poor and ignorant people—the majority indeed were illiterate—but there was hardly an instance of breach of the principles."[8]

Perhaps the greatest testimony of Gandhi's success as a Satyagrahi was the change of heart that was apparently brought about in the "so-called opponent", viz. General Smuts, head of the South African Government. V.P. Verma describes how Smuts became deeply conscious of the virtues of sincerity, unselfishness and humanism that he found in Gandhi. Here are Smut's words of recognition of Gandhi's greatness—"However often we may differ from him, we are conscious all the time of his sincerity, his unselfishness,and above all of his fundamental and universal humanity. He always acts as a great human, with deep sympathy for men of all classes and all races and especially for the under-dog."[9]

Two more applications of non-violent opposition, based on truth and fearlessness

3.13. Non-violent opposition to injustice, as illustrated in the preceding para, has unlimited scope in terms of applications, of which the following two are particularly noteworthy in the present context:

(a) against imperialism of any type

(b) against religious fanaticism.

For purposes of illustrating (a) the most well-known example is Gandhi's non-violent opposition to British rule in India during the years 1919-1947. Jawaharlal Nehru, Gandhi's closest colleague in this struggle, has visualized a link between Gandhi's approach and the Upanisadic exhortation to fearlessness. We first present a small part of the relevant conversation between the Philosopher Yajnavalkya and the action-oriented King Janaka, as given in Brihadaranyak Upanisad:

अभयं वै जनक प्राप्तोऽसि ।
इति होवाच याज्ञवल्क्यः ॥
स होवाच जनको वैदेहः ।
अभयं त्वा गच्छताद्याज्ञवल्क्य ।
यो नो भगवन् अभयं वेदयसे ।
इमे विदेहाः अयमहमस्मि ॥ वृहदारण्यक उप० 4.2.4

abhayaṁ vai janaka prāptosi
iti hovācha Yajñavalkyaḥ
sa hovācha janako vaidehaḥ
abhayaṁ tvā gacchatādyājnavalkya
yo no bhagvan abhayaṁ vedayase
ime videhāḥ ayamahamasmi

—*Brihadaranyak Up.* 4.2.4

Simple meaning—Yajnavalkya said, O Janaka, you have attained the fearless i.e. made fearlessness an integral part of your nature. The action-oriented King Janaka replied, O Venerable Yajnavalkya, the credit goes to your teaching. You have equated fearlessness with Brahman, and taught us both the philosophic and practical aspects of it. I and all the citizens of my kingdom are acting in accordance with your teaching.

And now, Nehru's analysis of this, in terms of the events that took place in India in the early 1920s: "Janaka and Yajnavalkya had said, at the dawn of our history, that it was the function of the leaders of a people to make them fearless. But the dominant impulse in India under British rule was that of fear—pervasive, oppressing, strangling fear; fear of the army, the police, the widespread secret service, fear of the official class; fear of laws meant to suppress and of prison; fear of the landlord's agent, fear of the moneylender; fear of unemployment and starvation, which were always on the threshold. It was against this all-pervading fear that Gandhi's quiet and determined voice was raised: Be not afraid."[10]

Next, the point (b) viz. non-violent opposition to religious fanaticism—this has assumed special significance in the twenty-first century.What it means in practice is, that the threat of punishment or fear of hell, which the religious fanatics misinterpret to frighten innocent people, as also the unjustified allurement of heaven promised to blind followers of fanaticism-both these need to be challenged by the fearless and peace-loving followers of the same faith, in the interest of peace everywhere. These challengers can draw support from the

Upanisads which are non-denominational and can be applied universally, exemplified by the following hymn:

यतो वा इमानि भूतानि जायन्ते
येन जातानि जीवन्ति ।
यत् प्रयंत्यभिसंविशन्ति
तत् विजिज्ञासस्व तत् ब्रह्मेति ॥ तैत्तिरीय उप० 3.1

yato vā imāni bhūtāni jāyante
yena jātāni jīvanti
yat prayantyabhisaṃvishanti
tat vijijnāsasva tat brahmeti —*Tattiriya Up.* 3.1

Simple meaning—The Ultimate Reality, from which all these entities and beings are born, that, in which, being born, they live, and that, unto which, in the end, they enter-Know That, That is Brahman.

Since all human beings have come out of Brahman (the Ultimate Reality) and they will go back into it, there is no justification to be afraid of hell, nor to be bribed (or allured) by a promise of heaven (as given to suicide bombers).

Reinforce the call for raising women's status in society, by referring to great women of the Upanisads

3.14. The call to recognize the equality of women with men is an obvious message of the Upanisads, as explained in the earlier paras. Furthermore, Brihadaranyak Upanisad and Chandogya Upanisad provide detailed information about three great women of those days-and this information can be utilized to re-affirm the call to raise women's status in the modern society. The names of these three great women are: Maitreyi, Gargi, and Jabālā.

Maitreyi, the wife of the great philosopher Yajnavalkya, received honor in the society. But, with the passage of time, Maitreyi herself became a great philosopher and received honor because of her own merit too. Brihadaranyak Upanisad describes how Yajnavalkya suggested that, due to advancing age, he may retire to the forest, leaving plenty of wealth for

Maitreyi to continue living comfortably in the same home as before. To this, Maitreyi replied:

येनाहं नामृता स्यां किमहं तेन कुर्याम् ।
यदेव भगवान्वेद तदेव मे ब्रूहीति ॥ बृहदारण्यक उप० 2.4.3

yenāhaṁ nāmritā syāṁ kimahaṁ tena
kuryām. yadeva bhagavānveda tadeva
me brūhīti —*Brihadaranyak Up.* 2.4.3

Simple meaning—Maitreyi said, O venerable well-wisher, you suggested that I may accept wealth and be happy. But my goal is higher than that - I want to attain the bliss of the knowledge of Brahman. Therefore, please impart to me the knowledge that you have, and then we may retire to the forest together.

Yajnavalkya was so happy to hear this, and he said:

प्रिया बतारे नः सती प्रियं भाषसे ।
एहि आस्स्व । व्याख्यास्यामि ते ॥ बृहदारण्यक उप० 2.4.4

priyā batāre naḥ satī priyaṁ bhāṣase
ehi āssva. vyākhyāsyāmi te
—*Brihadaranyak Up.* 2.4.4

Simple meaning—Yajnavalkya replied, my dear, I have always loved you, and now your sweet words have endeared you to me even more. I will certainly honor your wishes, and I will be glad to impart to you the knowledge that I have. Subsequently, we may retire to the forest together.

Gargi's greatness as a scholar is also narrated in Brihadaranyak Upanisad. Her status as a scholar was almost as high as that of Yajnavalkya. Groups of other scholars, before challenging Yajnavalkya to a contest of scholarship, used to seek the advice of Gargi, to check whether they were qualified enough to face Yajnavalkya. In one of the stories of Brihadaranyak Upanisad, Gargi told such a group of scholars:

ब्राह्मणा भगवन्तस्तदेव बहु मन्येध्वं
यदस्मान्नमस्कारेण मुच्येध्वम् ।
न वै जातु युस्माकमिमं कश्चिद् ब्रह्मोद्यं जेतेति ॥
बृहदारण्यक उप० 3.8.12

brāhmaṇā bhagavantastadeva bahu manyedhvaṁ
yadasmānnamaskāreṇa muchyedhvam
na vai jātu yusmākamimaṁ kashchid
brahmodyaṁ jeteti —*Brihadaranyak Up.* 3.8.12

Simple meaning—Gargi said, venerable brahmanas, my sincere advice to you is this—please go, meet him, and do namaskara (i.e. pay respect to him). But please give up the idea of challenging him, because none of you could possibly win.

And the scholars accepted Gargi's advice.

Jabala's greatness as a poor but wise mother is highlighted in Chandogya Upanisad. While sending her young son Satyakama to seek admission to the Ashrama of a famous teacher, she said, "Don't pretend that you come from a high class family—just tell the truth." And the teacher was highly impressed, and he said to Satyakama:

समिधं सोम्याहरोप त्वा नेष्ये ।
न सत्यादगा ॥ छन्दोग्य उप० 4.4.5

samidhaṁ somyāharopa tvā neṣye
na satyādagā —*Chandogya Up.* 4.4.5

Simple meaning—The teacher said, my dear Satyakama, you have satisfied me about your qualifications to join my āshrama because you have not deviated from truth. I grant you admission.

In due course of time, Satyakama himself became a famous teacher. But Chandogya Upanisad makes it clear that Satyakama's greatness was primarily due to the greatness of his mother (and this is reflected in his full name, viz. Satyakama Jabala which means, Satyakama, son of Jabala)

Let the concept of secular democracy be supported, in the interest of world peace

3.15. On the basis of the discussion already presented in the earlier paras, it can be inferred that the biggest contribution to world peace can be made by those countries that are secular democracies. Since the United Nations is exploring all possible ways of strengthening the cause of world peace, it may consider how more and more countries in the world could become secular democracies. Of course, the cooperation of the concerned governments will be needed for a peaceful change.

Swami Ranganathananda has studied the linkage between the Upanisads and Indian secularism. His broad conclusion is that Indian secularism is supported by the tolerant, all-embracing Upanisadic tradition.[11]

Three ways in which the Upanisadic message has been extended and applied, for strengthening the cause of world peace

3.16. The Upanisadic message has been extended and applied to a wide variety of problems. For our present purpose, we shall briefly refer to only three such instances:

(i) Sri Aurobindo extended the evolution-supporting approach of the Upanisads beyond the outline given in Chandogya Upanisad (reference para 3.4), for developing his theory of Spiritual Evolution and Purna-yoga, which can become instrumental in strengthening the cause of world peace. He views Spiritual Evolution as a continuation of the Biological Evolution which has seen the emergence of Life out of Matter, and of Mind out of Life. Whereas the Biological Evolution was a slow, natural process, Aurobindo believes that the Spiritual Evolution could be expedited by human effort. The special feature of Aurobindo's theory of Spiritual Evolution is the anticipated emergence of Supermind out of Mind. Once that state of spiritual perfection is attained, through Purna-yoga, the perfected person voluntarily comes down to the level of ordinary human beings and lifts them up, morally and spiritually. Purna-yogins (like Sri Aurobindo) are great contributors to world peace, and the greater the number of such persons in the world, the greater their contribution to world peace.[12]

(ii) Bhagavad-Gita extended the concept of nishkam karma-yoga beyond the outline given in Isha Upanisad, and helped produce karmayogins who have been working for world peace.

This will be explained in the next chapter. (Please see para 4.29)

(iii) Maharshi Mahesh Yogi extended the concept of meditation beyond the outline given in Muṇḍaka Upanisad (by adding thereto Patanjali's Yoga-Sutra) to develop his theory of Applying Meditation to the Cause of World Peace. We are not presenting here details regarding this meditation-oriented approach, because our coverage in this book is confined to action-oriented approaches to world peace.

CHAPTER 4

Bhagavad-Gita's Identification of Peace-Breakers and Call for Preventive Action

4.1 The last two chapters have given details about the Vedic message of peace and the strengthening thereof by the Upanisadic philosophy of oneness of all human beings. The history of those times tells us that while many people acted in accordance with this message, some did not. Bhagavad-Gita (or Gita for short) therefore felt it necessary to add a new dimension to what was done earlier on this subject, and this new approach was centered on two steps which are outlined in the following two verses (composed by us):

एकत्वं सर्वभूतेषु ज्ञातव्यं श्रुतिमंत्रेभ्यः ।
शान्तिसंस्थापनार्थाय ज्ञातव्यं पृथक्त्वमपि ॥
शान्तिभंगो न हि भवेत् प्रयासं के करिष्यन्ति ।
लोकसंग्रहसंलग्ना निष्कामकर्मयोगिनः ॥

ekatvaṁ sarvabhūteṣu jnātavyaṁ shrutimantrebhyaḥ
shāntisamsthāpanārthāya jnātavyaṁ prithaktvamapi
shāntibhango na hi bhavet prayāsaṁ ke kariṣyanti
lokasamgrahasamlagnā nishkāmakarmayoginaḥ

Simple meaning—The first new step taken by the Bhagavad-Gita was to emphasize that, side by side with the acquisition of the knowledge of oneness of all human beings, it was essential to know about those people also who did not believe in oneness (ekatvam), because their own philosophy of separateness (prithaktvam) would prompt them to be peace-breakers.

The second new step taken by the Bhagavad-Gita to support the cause of peace was to envisage that peace-promoters (Karmayogins) would voluntarily work for lokasamgraha (which means good of the world and therefore includes world peace) and thus try to prevent the breaking of peace. In both the cases, the Gita took the Upanisads' message as the starting point but developed new concepts as well as new terminology.

4.2. Accordingly the present chapter will consist of three main sections:

(a) Identification of peace-breakers,

(b) Developing the concepts of Karmayoga, Karmayogins, and Lokasamgraha

(c) Applications of Gita's ideas.

Identification of peace-breakers

4.3. The concept of right knowledge which upholds peace, and which the Gita has stated repeatedly, is obviously based on the Upanisads:

सर्वभूतेषु येनैकं भावमव्ययमीक्षते ।
अविभक्तं विभक्तेषु तज्ज्ञानं विद्धि सात्त्विकम् ॥ 18.20 ॥

sarvabhūteṣu yenaikaṁ bhāvamavyayamīksate
avibhaktaṁ vibhhakteṣu tajjñānaṁ viddhi sāttvikam
—18.20

Simple meaning—Through right knowledge, one sees the same Brahman in every human being. Through such knowledge, one establishes unity among apparently different beings.

4.4. After looking at the instances when peace was broken, Bhagavad-Gita drew attention to those who were responsible for breaking peace:

एतां दृष्टिमवष्टभ्य नष्टात्मानोऽल्पबुद्धयः ।
प्रभवन्त्युग्रकर्माण : क्षयाय जगतोऽहिता: ॥ 16.9 ॥

etāṁ driṣṭimavaṣṭabhya naṣṭātmānolpabuddhayaḥ
prabhavantyugrakarmāṇaḥ ksayāya jagatohitāḥ
—16.9

Simple meaning—Narrow-minded people, who do not have the right knowledge, are anti-social and self-destructive too. They commit violent acts which harm the society and can even destroy the world.

4.5. Bhagavad-Gita further analysed in detail the mental make-up of the peace-breakers.While quoting below the relevant verses of the Gita, it was felt appropriate in a couple of cases, to change slightly the terminology so as to make them relevant to the peace-breaking problem. In order to achieve further simplification, some verses from other sources have also been included.

4.6. अधर्मं धर्ममिति या मन्यते तमसावृता ।
सर्वार्थान् विपरीतांश्च बुद्धिः सा पार्थ तामसी ॥ 18.32

adharmaṁ dharmamiti yā manyate tamasāvritā
sarvārthān viparītāṁshcha buddhiḥ sā pārtha tāmasī
—18.32

Simple meaning—Peace-breakers have a perverted value system, and an anti-social mentality. Therefore their concept of religion is just the opposite of what religion really is.

4.7. असौ मया हतः शत्रुः हनिष्ये चापरानपि ।
ईश्वरोऽहमहं भोगी सिद्धोऽहं बलवान्सुखी ॥ 16.14

asau mayā hataḥ shatruḥ hanişye chāparānapi
īshvarohamahaṁ bhogī siddhohaṁ balavānsukhī
—16.14

Simple meaning—These people commit themselves to violence, and killing of innocent persons, one after another, is their main job. They think that, by so doing, they will establish their supremacy over every one else, and that this will make them happy.

4.8. मूढग्राहेणात्मनो यत्पीडया क्रियते तप : ।
परस्योत्सादनार्थं वा तत्तामसमुदाहृतम् ॥ 17.19

mūḍhagrāheṇātmano yatpīdayā kriyate tapaḥ
parasyotsādanārthaṁ vā tattāmasamudāhritam
—17.19

Simple meaning—These people have a closed mind and they do not realize the folly which is prompting them to kill others, but which, at the same time, is harming themselves too.

4.9. घर्मयुद्धभ्रमासक्ता मोहजालसमावृता: ।
गृहीत्वा हि मिथ्याभेगान् हिंसाप्रदिग्धान् नान्यथा ॥

dharmayuddhabhramāsaktā mohajālasamāvritāḥ
grihītvā hi mithyābhogān himsāpradigdhān nānyathā

Simple meaning—These people are swayed by an illusion that they are fighting a holy war and they do not realize that the glory and pleasures that they are seeking are drenched in the blood of innocent citizens of the world, and therefore are no pleasures at all.

4.10. आढ्योऽभिजनवानस्मि कोऽन्योस्ति सदृशो मया ।
यक्ष्ये दास्यामि मोदिस्य इत्यज्ञानविमोहिता: ॥ 16.15

āḍhyobhijanavānasmi konyosti sadrisho mayā
yaksye dāsyāmi modisya ityajñānavimohitāḥ
—16.15

Simple meaning—These people boast about the enormous money that they command, and try to gain popularity by offering money to fake charities as well as to potential peace-breakers, without realizing that their tricks are now being exposed.

4.11. आत्मसम्भाविता: स्तब्धा धनमानमदान्विता: ।
यजन्ते नामयज्ञैस्ते दम्भेन च भयावहै: ॥ 16.17

ātmasambhāvitāḥ stabdhā dhanamānamadānvitāḥ
yajante nāmayajnaiste dambhena cha bhayāvahaiḥ
—16.17

Simple meaning—These people are self-conceited and haughty. They are under an illusion that so many people honor them, without realizing that such expression of honor is because of fear. Their donations to charities are mainly to hide their real intensions.

4.12. संदिग्धख्यातिलोभस्तु वास्तविक: प्रयोजन: ।
घर्मध्वज: नाममात्रं अनेकविद्वत्सम्मते ॥

sandigdhakhyātilobhastu vāstavikaḥ prayojanaḥ
dharmadhvajaḥ nāmamātraṁ anekavidvatsammate

Simple meaning—These people are trying to hide the fact that their real intention is to acquire fame, without realizing that such fame is, in essence, notoriety. The fact that their championship of religion is fraudulent, is now being exposed.

4.13. इदमद्य मया लब्धमिदं प्राप्स्ये मनोरथं ।
इदमस्तीदमपि मे भविष्यति पुनर्धनम् ॥ 16.13

idamadya mayā labdhamidaṁ prāpsye manoratham
idamastīdamapi me bhaviṣyati punardhanam
—16.13

Simple meaning—These people keep on expanding their evil designs. With the passage of time, their intrigues and greed show no sign of slowing down.

4.14. अदेशकाले यद्दानं अपात्रेभ्यश्च दीयते ।
त्यक्तनीतिसंविधानं तत्तामसमुदाहृतम् ॥ 17.22

adeshakāle yaddānaṁ apātrebhyashca dīyate
tyaktanītisamvidhānaṁ tattāmasamudāhritam
—17.22

Simple meaning—The flow of funds to such people also shows no sign of slowing down because anti-social elements in the society keep on donating to unrighteous organizations, bypassing rules and regulations.

4.15. अहंकारं बलं दर्पं कामं क्रोधं च संश्रिता: ।
मामात्मपरदेहेषु प्रद्विषन्तोऽभ्यसूयका: ॥ 16.18

ahaṃkāraṁ balaṁ darpaṁ kāmaṁ krodhaṁ cha samshritāḥ
māmātmaparadeheṣu pradviṣantobhyasūyakāḥ
—16.18

Simple meaning—In this way, the arrogance, violence and cruelty of these people go on spreading hatred, jealousy and intolerance.

4.16. पृथक्त्वेन तु यज्ज्ञानं नानाभावान्पृथग्विधान् ।
वेत्ति सर्वेषु भूतेषु तज्ज्ञानं नाशकारकम् ॥ 18.21

prithaktvena tu yajjnānaṁ nānābhāvānprithagvidhān
vetti sarveṣu bhūteṣu tajjñānaṁ nāshakārakam
—18.21

Simple meaning—The main reason why these people are engaged in destructive activities is that they do not believe in the oneness of all human beings—in other words, their philosophy of separateness is the root cause of the problem.

4.17. अयं निजः परो वेति गणना लघुचेतसाम् ।
तेषां मते भ्रातृभावः स्वजनायैव सीमितः ॥

ayaṁ nijaḥ paro veti gaṇanā laghuchetasām
teṣāṁ mate bhrātribhāvaḥ svajanāyaiva sīmitaḥ

Simple meaning—These people, being narrow-minded, divide the society into friends and foes. Although they claim that they believe in brotherhood, yet it is clear that such a feeling is only towards their own people (and hence limited), not towards all the members of the society.

4.18. अवजानन्ति मां मूढा मानुषीं तनुमाश्रितम् ।
परं भावमजानन्तो मम भूतमहेश्वरम् ॥ 9.11

avajānanti māṁ muḍhā mānuṣīṁ tanumāshritam
paraṁ bhāvamajānanto mama bhūtamaheshvaram

Simple meaning—The reason why these people divide the society into friends and foes is linked to their narrow (exclusive) belief—they do not believe that an element of divinity is in every human being. If they had such an inclusive, peace-promoting belief, then they would not look down upon any human being (male or female).

4.19. प्रवृत्तिं च निवृत्तिं च जना न विदुरासुराः ।
न शौचं नापि चाचारो न सत्यं तेषु विद्यते ॥ 16.7

pravrittim̐ cha nivrittim̐ cha janā na vidurāsurāḥ
na shoucham̐ nāpi chāchāro na satyam̐ teṣu vidyate
—16.7

Simple meaning—Since these people do not have the right (inclusive) belief, they are unable to take the right decision as to what is doable and what is non-doable. Therefore, their conduct is anti-social, being based on untruth (exclusive belief).

14.20. अनुबन्धं क्षयं हिंसामनवेक्ष्य च पौरुषम् ।
मोहादारभ्यते कर्म यत्तत्तामसमुच्यते ॥ 18.25

anubandham̐ ksayam̐ him̐sāmanaveksya ca pauruṣam
mohādārabhyate karma yattattāmasamucyate
—18.25

Simple meaning—Since these people are unable to take the right decision, they commit themselves to violence and destruction, and they over-estimate their own strength, thus causing too much destruction, because of which the world has to take protective measures.

4.21. दम्भो दर्पोऽतिमानश्च क्रोधः पारुष्यमेव च ।
अज्ञानं चाभिजातस्य पार्थ सम्पदमासुरीम् ॥ 16.4

dambho darpotimānashca krodhaḥ pāruṣyameva ca
ajñānam̐ cābhijātasya pārtha sampadamāsurīm
—16.4

Simple meaning—The root cause of all the anti-social actions of the peace-breakers (interlinked with their cruelty, arrogance, etc.) is the lack of right knowledge or of right education.

4.22. धर्मग्रन्थं कथयन्तः किं त्वाश्रिता भेदभावम् ।
संलग्नाः क्रूरकर्मणि कथमेतद् धर्मज्ञानम् ॥

dharmagrantham̐ kathayantaḥ kim̐ tvāshritā bhedabhāvam
samlagnāḥ krūrakarmaṇi kathametad dharmajnānam

Simple meaning—These people claim that they have full knowledge, particularly religious knowledge. Therefore, two messages must be conveyed to them. How can they divide the human society into two groups—friends and foes? And how can they commit violence against the so-called foes? These are the real tests of religious knowledge, not their ability to quote from their religious text.

Developing the concepts of Karmayoga, Karmayogins, and Lokasamgraha

4.23. As in the preceding section (i.e. from para 4.3 on), here too the Gita took the Upanisads' message as the starting point. Specifically, the first two hymns of Isha Upanisad,written below, formed the base on which the Gita developed the concepts of karmayoga, karmayogins, and lokasamgraha:

ईशा वास्यं इदं सर्वं यत्किंच जगत्यां जगत् ।
तेन त्यक्तेन भुंजीथा मा गृधः कस्यस्विद्धनम् ॥
कुर्वन्नेह कर्माणि जिजीविषेत् शतं समाः ।
एवं त्वयि नान्यथेतोऽस्ति न कर्म लिप्यते नरे ॥ –ईशा. उप. 1.1-2

īshā vāsyaṁ idaṁ sarvaṁ yatkinca jagatyāṁ jagat
tena tyaktena bhunjīthā mā gridhaḥ kasyasviddhanam
kurvanneveha karmāṇi jijīviṣet shatam samāḥ
evaṁ tvayi nānyathetosti na karma lipyate nare

—*Isha Upanisad* 1.1-2

Simple meaning—Brahman is in every human being. Brahman has provided enough of useful things to meet every one's needs. It is advisable not to grab anything from any one. Rather, one who is willing to give, if necessary, will feel happier.

In this world, one should desire to live a hundred years, but only by performing socially useful actions. Thus, and in no other way, can a person be free from the bondage which anti-social action will cause.

4.24. The three terms of the Gita, viz. Karmayoga, Karmayogins, and Lokasamgraha, are closely inter-linked, and therefore their meaning and significance can be best clarified, not one-by-one, but taking all three together. To start with Karmayoga, its meaning is, the right technique of performing actions. However, it must be clarified that the complete expression for such a technique is 'nishkam karmayoga' which stands for the technique of performing socially useful actions, without any desire to make selfish gains. In other words, karmayoga is essentially an abridgement of 'nishkam karmayoga'. Here the reference to socially useful actions links karmayoga to lokasamgraha, which (literally meaning 'good of the world') signifies the purpose of karmayoga. Finally, the expression 'karmayogins' denotes those persons (male or female, and similarly with no other restriction) who perform socially useful actions, with the purpose of achieving lokasamgraha, and who make use of the technique of nishkam karmayoga.

4.25. From the point of view of Gita's contribution to world peace, the center of attention has to be lokasamgraha. The Gita itself has given the message of lokasamgraha from as many as ten angles. This may look surprising because traditional commentators did not explain the Gita from the lokasamgraha perspective. The approach of this chapter is obviously lokasamgraha-centered because otherwise it cannot extract from the Gita, its message of peace, on the basis of which the peace-promoters (karmayogins) can try to strengthen the global search for peace. However, in order to restrict the size of this chapter, while still presenting all the ten angles, we will make each of these presentations as short as possible.

4.26. Linking lokasamgraha to Vedic Yajna. In chapter 3 of the Gita, the message of lokasamgraha has been derived from the Vedic yajna (reference paras 2.42 and 2.55). The following verses present a summarized version of Gita's ideas on this topic (and to obtain a clear statement from the minimum possible number of verses, we had to include one of the familiar harmonizing verses):

नियतं कुरु कर्म त्वं कर्म ज्यायो ह्यकर्मणः ।
शरीरयात्रापि च ते न प्रसिद्ध्येदकर्मणः ॥ 3.8
सहयज्ञाः प्रजाः सृष्ट्वा पुरोवाच प्रजापतिः ।
अनेन प्रसविष्यध्वमेष वोऽस्त्विष्टकामधुक् ॥ 3.10
इदं न मम मंत्रेण त्यागभावना दर्शिता ।

तेन त्यक्तेन भुंजीथा: तदेव ज्ञानं दर्शितम् ॥
एवं प्रवर्तितं चक्रं नानुवर्तयतीह य: ।
अघायुरिन्द्रियारामो मोघं पार्थ स जीवति ॥ 3.16

niyataṁ kuru karma tvaṁ karma jyāyo hyakarmanaḥ
sharīrayātrāpi ca te na prasiddhyedakarmaṇaḥ —3.8
sahayajnāḥ prajāḥ sriṣṭvā purovāca prajāpatiḥ
anena prasaviṣyadhvameṣa vostviṣṭakāmadhuk —3.10
idaṁ na mama mantreṇa tyāgabhāvanā darshitā
tena tyaktena bhunjīthāḥ tadeva jnānaṁ darshitam
evaṁ pravartitaṁ cakraṁ nānuvartayatīha yaḥ
aghāyurindriyārāmo moghaṁ pārtha sa jīvati—3.16

Simple meaning—Perform actions with the right spirit prescribed by the Vedas, i.e. the spirit of sacrifice. Otherwise your life in this world will become purposeless.

The Creator advised all human beings, from the very beginning, to work with the yajna-spirit , in the interest of every one's progress as well as acquisition of desired objects for all.

Remember that while performing yajna, the Vedic scholar uttered the words 'idam na mama'(i.e. this is not mine), which clearly gave a message of sacrifice. The same message was conveyed by the Upanisads also, viz. that one who is willing to give, will feel happier.

Therefore, don't let those messages be forgotten. Keep up the yajna-spirit and maintain the entire society on the path of co-operation and progress, remembering all the time the principle of helping one another.

4.27. Extending katha upanisad. The important concept of Shreyas (meaning liberation) was formulated by katha upanisad. Its extension to lokasamgraha is achieved in the third chapter of the Gita, through the following dialogue between Arjuna and Lord Krishna. Arjuna asks how he can attain Shreyas:

तदेकं वद निश्चित्य येन श्रेयोऽहमाप्नुयाम् ॥ 3.2
श्रेय: कठोपनिषदि पुनश्च हरिगीतके ।
पर्यायवाची मोक्षस्य तथा भिन्नं च प्रेयस: ॥

tadekaṁ vada nishcitya yena shreyohamāpnuyām 3.2
shreyaḥ kaṭhopaniṣadi punashca harigītake
paryāyavācī mokṣasya tathā bhinnam ca preyasaḥ

Simple meaning—Arjuna says, please tell me one definite way which will take me to shreyas (liberation). Obviously, he is referring here to Katha Upanisad which had formulated the concepts of preyas (pleasant) and Shreyas (highest good *i.e.* liberation).

In reply, Krishna tells Arjuna that the definite way to reach Shreyas is lokasamgraha:

परस्परं भावयन्त: श्रेय: परमवाप्स्यथ ॥ 3.11
श्रेयोऽर्थं नरजीवनं साधनं लोकसंग्रह: ।
लोकसंग्रहे येनैव श्रेयो दृष्टं स दर्शक: ॥

parasparaṁ bhāvayantaḥ shreyaḥ
paramavāpsyatha. 3.11
shreyorthaṁ narajīvanaṁ sādhanaṁ
lokasamgrahaḥ
lokasamgrahe yenaiva shreyo driṣṭaṁ
sa darshakaḥ

Simple meaning—Lord Krishna says, by helping one another, all of you will definitely attain shreyas (liberation). This means that the goal of shreyas can not be reached if one tries to go to it directly, because the definite way to shreyas is indirect, *i.e.* through lokasamgraha. In fact, one's whole-hearted effort should be to work for lokasamgraha (good of all), and then Shreyas will automatically follow.

4.28. Lokasamgraha as repayment of debt. The Gita tells human beings that all their capabilities are developed with the support of their families and of the whole society. Therefore,when they grow up and become capable, they should voluntarily repay the debt i.e. help all the members of the society to the best of their ability.

> यद्यद् विभूतिमत्सत्त्वं श्रीमदूर्जितमेव वा ।
> तत्तदेवावगच्छ त्वं मम तेजोंऽशसंभवम् ॥ 10.41
> तैर्दत्तान् अप्रदायैभ्यो यो भुंक्ते स्तेन एव सः ॥ 3.12
>
> *yadyad vibhūtimatsattvaṁ shrīmadūrjitameva vā*
> *tattadevāvagaccha tvaṁ mama tejoṁshasambhavam*
> —10.41
> *tairdattān apradāyaibhyo yo bhunkte stena eva saḥ*
> —3.12

Simple meaning—Lord Krishna tells Arjuna, you should be aware that, God, operating through human beings, helps all the members of the society to develop their capabilities. In other words, every human being is indebted to the society (and to God). If any member of the society, after growing up, does not repay the debt to the society (i.e. does not help other members of the society), then that person is like a thief. Thus the desire to repay the debt to the society leads one to lokasamgraha.

4.29. Lokasamgraha arises from sympathy and philosophic equality. The message of philosophic equality of all human beings was given by the Upanisads. The Gita argued that, in the interest of universal welfare, the feeling of equality must be supplemented with sympathy. Chapters six and seventeen of the Gita convey this message (and again we have to modify one of the verses to squeeze into it the complete message):

> आत्मौपम्येन सर्वत्र समं पश्यति योऽर्जुन ।
> सुखं वा यदि वा दुःखं स योगी परमो मतः ॥ 6.32
> आत्मौपम्येन भावेन सहानुभूतिः सर्वेषु ।
> अहिंसा संविभागं च वाक्यं प्रियहितं तथा ॥ 17.15
>
> *ātmaupamyena sarvatra samaṁ pashyati yorjuna*
> *sukhaṁ vā yadi vā duhkhaṁ sa yogī paramo mataḥ*
> —6.32
> *ātmaupamyena bhāvena sahānubhūtiḥ sarveṣu*

ahimsā samvibhāgaṁ ca vākyaṁ priyahitaṁ tathā
—17.15

Simple meaning—Since every human being has the same Atman (Self), they are all essentially equal. But along with the feeling of equality, the peace-promoter (yogin) also has sympathy, *i.e.* feeling happy when others are happy, and feeling unhappy when others are unhappy. Other virtues that go along with equality and sympathy are: non-violence, sharing, and use of sweet and helpful words.

4.30. Lokasamgraha as a corrective to group loyalty. The first chapter of the Gita depicts Arjuna as a believer in group loyalty (svajana—raksa), but after listening to Lord Krishna, Arjuna gives up group loyalty in favour of Lokasamgraha. In order to summarize all this in three and a half verses, we present below a mixture of Gita-verses from chapter one, and two other verses that condense several chapters and culminate in chapter twelve:

तस्मान्नार्हा वयं हन्तुं धार्तराष्ट्रान् स्वबांधवान् ।
स्वजनं हि कथं हत्वा सुखिनः स्याम माधव ॥ 1.37
पापमेवाश्रयेदस्मान् हत्वैतानाततायिनः ॥ 1.36
अपूर्णा स्वजनरक्षा विना हि लक्ष्यविस्तारात् ।
लक्ष्ये च तस्याः पूर्णत्वं प्राप्तव्यं लोकसंग्रहे ॥
केवलं स्वजनरक्षा द्वेषभावोऽन्यभूतेभ्यः ।
त्यजन्ति स्वजनरक्षां सर्वभूतहितेरताः ॥ 12.4

tasmānnārha vayaṁ hantuṁ dhārtarāṣṭrān svabāndhavān
svajanam hi katham hatvā sukhinaḥ syāma mādhava
—1.37
pāpamevāshrayedasmān hatvaitānātatāyinaḥ
—1.36
apūrṇā svajanaraksā vinā hi laksyavistārāt laksye
ca tasyāḥ pūrṇatvaṁ prāptavyaṁ lokasamgrahe
kevalaṁ svajanarakṣā dveṣabhāvonyabhūtebhyaḥ
tyajanti svajanaraksāṁ sarvabhūtahite ratāḥ
—12.4

Simple meaning—Arjuna says (in chapter one of the Gita) that, although I know that Duryodhana's supporters are criminals, still I feel that I should protect them because they are my relations, my people. Lord Krishna tells Arjuna that, when there is a conflict between group loyalty and good of all (lokasamgraha), then group loyalty must have a lower priority than good of all, particularly if group loyalty is accompanied with hatred towards other people. That is why, those working for lokasamgraha have to go beyond group loyalty (when it is contrary to good of all). The closing words of this message of Lord Krishna occur in chapter twelve of the Gita. It should be added that, after listening to Lord Krishna, Arjuna too accepts lokasamgraha as a corrective to group loyalty.

4.31. Lokasamgraha as a healer of fragmentation wounds. Chapter eighteen of the Gita says that destructive activities are undertaken by those people who do not have the right knowledge about the oneness of all human beings. As a cure, chapter four says that the surest way to prevent destruction is to facilitate the acquisition of right knowledge by the peace-breakers. We present below four verses, selected from chapters eighteen and four (modifying one of them slightly):

पृथक्त्वेन तु यज्ज्ञानं नानाभावान्पृथग्विधान् ।
वेत्ति सर्वेषु भूतेषु तज्ज्ञानं नाशकारकम् ॥ 18.21
तद्विद्धि प्रणिपातेन परिप्रश्नेन सेवया ।
उपदेक्ष्यन्ति ते ज्ञानं ज्ञानिनस्तत्त्वदर्शिनः ॥ 4.34
यज्ज्ञात्वा न पुनर्मोहं एवं यास्यसि पाण्डव ।
येन भूतान्यशेषेण द्रक्ष्यस्यात्मन्यथो मयि ॥ 4.35
अपि चेदसि पापेभ्यः सर्वेभ्यः पापकृत्तमः ।
सर्वं ज्ञानप्लवेनैव वृजिनं सन्तरिष्यसि ॥ 4.36

prithaktvena tu yajjnānaṁ nānābhāvānprithagvidhān
vetti sarveṣu bhūteṣu tajjñānaṁ nāṣhakārakam —18.21
tadviddhi praṇipātena pariprashnena sevayā
upadekṣyanti te jnānaṁ jnāninastattvadarshinaḥ—4.34
yajjñātvā na punarmohaṁ evaṁ yāsyasi pāṇḍava

yena bhūtanyasheṣeṇa draksyasyātmanyatho mayi
—4.35

api cedasi pāpebhyaḥ sarvebhyaḥ pāpakrittamaḥ
sarvaṁ jñānaplavenaiva vrijinaṁ santariṣyasi —4.36

Simple meaning—The main reason why peace-breakers are engaged in destructive activities is that they do not believe in the oneness of all human beings—in other words, their philosophy of separateness is the root cause of the problem. As a cure, arrangements should be made so that these people can acquire the right knowledge. The process of gaining knowledge will be smooth if they have the desire to serve people (i.e. lokasamgraha), if they have an open mind, and if they can ask questions freely and politely. But once they go through this process and get the right knowledge, they will understand that all human beings are essentially one, and then they will give up group loyalty and become peace-loving citizens of the world. In this way, the fragmentation wounds (even the most serious ones) will be healed.

4.32. Lokasamgraha as a catalyst for transforming values. So far, the value system in our society has generally given priority to individual gains as compared to social gains. Because of the crisis situation that has thus been created, time is ripe to transform the value system so as to give the highest priority to lokasamgraha. The Gita has stressed, in chapters four and seventeen, the need to adjust priorities to changes in time, place and circumstances. Chapter twelve lists virtues (headed by lokasamgraha) which need to be given the highest priority today (and we have modified it slightly to specifically mention world peace):

स कालेनेह महता योगो नष्टः परन्तप ॥ 4.2
देशे काले च पात्रे च तद्दानं सात्त्विकं स्मृतम् ॥ 17.20
अद्वेष्टा सर्वभूतानां मैत्रः करुण एव च ।
निर्ममो निरहंकारः विश्वशान्तिप्रियः क्षमी ॥ 12.13

sa kāleneha mahatā yogo naṣṭaḥ parantapa —4.2

deshe kāle ca pātre ca taddānaṁ sāttvikaṁ smritam —17.20

adveṣṭā sarvabhūtānāṁ maitraḥ karuṇa eva ca
nirmamo nirahaṁkāraḥ vishvashāntipriyaḥ ksamī —12.13

Simple meaning—Whatever religious practice is started, parts of it become irrelevant after a long lapse of time. Therefore, it would be the right decision to make adjustments, in tune with changes in time, place and circumstances. The same considerations apply to the value system. Time is now ripe to transform the value system so as to give the highest priority to world peace. Along with that, friendliness, compassion, unselfishness, and polite behaviour should also be given due importance.

4.33. Lokasamgraha interlinked with pluralistic society. The Gita has declared that every individual has the right to choose the way of worshipping God so long as no pressure is exerted on others. Acceptance of this right is the basis of a pluralistic society which facilitates the voluntary involvement of people in lokasamgraha—activities. The Gita's message about freedom of choice is given in chapter four, and about sva-dharma (freely chosen path) in chapter three:

ये यथा मां प्रपद्यन्ते तांस्तथैव भजाम्यहम्।
मम वर्त्मानुवर्तन्ते मनुष्या: पार्थ सर्वश: ॥ 4.11
श्रेयान् स्वधर्मो विगुण: परधर्मात् स्वनुष्ठितात् ।
स्वधर्मे निधनं श्रेय: परधर्मो भयावह: ॥ 3.35

ye yathā māṁ prapadyante tāṁstathaiva bhajāmyaham
mam vartmānuvartante manusyāḥ partha sarvashaḥ —4.11

shreyān svadharmo viguṇaḥ paradharmāt svanuṣṭhitāt
svadharme nidhanaṁ shreyaḥ paradharmo bhayāvahaḥ —3.35

Simple meaning—Lord Krishna, as God, declares in the Gita, "Whosoever worships Me, through whatever path, I accept him (or her); all persons are moving along paths which in the end lead to Me." The faith freely chosen by any individual is fine for that person-and no attempt should be made to convert any one to a different faith. If these principles are followed everywhere, that would discourage peace-breakers from creating trouble.

4.34. Lokasamgraha as participation in God's work. The Gita says in chapter three that the biggest example of lokasamgraha is set by God who is constantly watching whether the world and all its citizens are safe, sound and happy. Whosoever amongst the human beings is voluntarily engaged in lokasamgraha-activities, is participating in God's work. After developing this idea in the chapters that follow, the Gita specifically says in chapter eleven that 'to be friendly with all' is the most important thing that lokasamgraha-activists can do. We present below the two relevant verses (one of them in a slightly modified form) together with a verse that condenses the intervening chapters (i.e. between the third and the eleventh):

उत्सीदेयुरिमे लोका न कुर्यां कर्म चेदहम् ।
विनाशस्य च कर्ता स्यामुपहन्यामिमाः प्रजाः ॥ 3.24
ईश्वरेणैव रक्षिताः तत्कर्म लोकसंग्रहः ।
लघुदीर्घभेदाद्विना यत्नो वांछितः सर्वेषाम् ॥
मत्कर्मकृन्मत्परमो मद्भक्तः संगवर्जितः ।
निर्वैरः सर्वभूतेषु यः स मामेति पाण्डव ॥ 11.55

utsīdeyurime lokā na kuryāṁ karma cedaham
vināśasya ca kartā syāmupahanyāmimāḥ prajāḥ
—3.24

īśvareṇaiva raksitāḥ tatkarma lokasaṁgrahaḥ
laghudīrghabhedādvinā yatno vānchitaḥ sarveṣām
matkarmakrinmatparamô madbhaktaḥ sangavarjitaḥ
nirvairaḥ sarvabhūteṣu yaḥ sa māmeti pāṇḍava
—11.55

Simple meaning—Lord Krishna, as God, says, "I constantly maintain a watch as to how the world and all its citizens are faring. This is my spontaneous activity because otherwise the world and all the people might be destroyed." This is the biggest example of lokasamgraha and it is the duty of all the people to participate in God's work i.e. lokasamgraha. Those who do so are karmayogins and the most important thing that they can do is to be friendly with all (and also to be environment-friendly).

4.35. Lokasamgraha as exemplified by karmayogins like Janaka. In order to clarify further what lokasamgraha means, the Gita gives, in chapter three, the example of the famous king Janaka of ancient India. We present here the relevant verse of the Gita, and in order to specify what type of work Janaka did, we also bring in here a verse from the Mahabharata.

कर्मणैव हि संसिद्धिमास्थिता जनकादय: ।
लोकसंग्रहमेवापि संपश्यन् कर्तुमर्हसि ॥ 3.20
देवेभ्यश्च पितृभ्यश्च भूतेभ्योऽतिथिभि: सह ।
इत्यर्थं सर्व एवेति समारम्भा भवन्ति वै ॥ महाभारत 14.32.24

karmaṇaiva hi samsiddhimāsthitā janakādayaḥ
lokasamgrahamevāpi sampasyan kartumarhasi
—3.20
devebhyasca pitribhyasca bhutebhyotithibhiḥ saha
ityartham sarva eveti samārambhā bhavanti vai
—*Mahabharata* 14.32.24

Simple meaning—Lord Krishna says to Arjuna, "This message of lokasamgraha which I am giving to you has been exemplified by Janaka and other karmayogins." The Gita does not give further information about Janaka, so a reference to Mahabharata is necessary. In the Mahabharata, Janaka says, "My activities are aimed to do good to all—including gods, ancestors, visitors and all other beings."

4.36. Having completed the presentation of lokasamgraha from all the ten angles, we now move on to karmayogins. The general meaning of karmayogins has already been indicated in para 4.24, viz. that they are any of the normal human beings (i.e. male or female, and similarly not subject to any other restriction) who perform socially useful actions, with the purpose of achieving lokasamgraha,and who make use of the technique of nishkam karmayoga. But the Gita has given detailed descriptions of karmayogins, on the basis of which we shall make short presentations on six points, viz.

(a) How capable and reliable are they as lokasamgraha-activists?

(b) Difference between those who work for lokasamgraha as 'duty-bound' and those who do so spontaneously.

(c) To have the protective and reformative capability, in the face of the anti-social traits of the peace-breakers, what are the peace-promoting virtues of the karmayogins?

(d) What knowledge, in addition to upanisadic knowledge, can contribute to the success of karmayogins?

(e) Difference between those who use meditation only to the extent needed, and those who give meditation a higher priority.

(f) Can monks too be karmayogins, like householders?

4.37. Capability of karmayogins. The Gita has made it clear that there is no intrinsic limit to what karmayogins could possibly do. In fact, the Gita has already been applied several times to conduct peaceful struggles for human rights (some of them will be briefly referred to in the closing section of this chapter). On the basis of those struggles, we have composed the following verse:

यदा यदा जनवर्गा भेदत्रस्ता निराश्रयाः ।
तदागमन्गीताभक्ता रक्षार्थं तेषामन्यायात् ॥

yadā yadā janavargā bhedatrastā nirāśrayāḥ
tadāgamangītābhaktā raksārthaṁ teṣāmanyāyāt

Simple meaning—When groups of helpless people faced discrimination and injustice, then (in several cases)the lokasamgraha activists volunteered to help them.

However, problems of world peace are obviously more challenging. If and when, any of the karmayogins voluntarily accept that challenge, they will need to keep in mind the following verse of the Gita:

अधिष्ठानं तथा कर्ता करणं च पृथग्विधम् ।
विविधाश्च पृथक्चेष्टा दैवं चैवात्र पंचमम् ॥ 18.14

adhiṣṭhānaṁ tathā kartā karaṇaṁ ca prithagvidham
vividhāśca prithakceṣṭā daivam caivātra pancamam
—18.14

Simple meaning—Lord Krishna says to Arjuna, "Before accepting any big challenge, carefully consider five points, viz. how difficult is the field of work, how capable you are, what resources you will have and through whom you will work, what will be your plan of work, and fifthly, remember the chance factor (i.e that chances of success cannot be hundred per cent)."

As to the third point i.e. resources and through whom work relating to world peace can be done, the obvious answer is "Through the United Nations."

In spite of the precautionary message stated above, the confidence that we have in karmayogins, is reflected in the following verse:

विश्वशान्तिप्रयत्नेषु संलग्नाः कर्मयोगिनः ।
न करिष्यन्ति तत्कर्म येन यत्नत्यागो भवेत् ॥

visvaśāntiprayatneṣu saṁlagnāḥ karmayoginaḥ
na kariṣyanti tatkarma yena yatnatyāgo bhavet

Simple meaning—If and when, any of the karmayogins voluntarily accept the challenge and start actively working for world peace, then they should be able to maintain that work for a very long time (i.e. they won't give up).

4.38. Duty-bound or spontaneous. If and when the karmayogins decide to make a significant contribution to world peace, they will have to ensure that volunteers from different countries come forward in large numbers. For this, it will be necessary to have short-term training courses, suitable for persons coming from different cultural background. Support for such a move can be found from the following verse of the Gita:

> आरुरुक्षोर्मुनेर्योगं कर्म कारणमुच्यते ।
> योगारूढस्य तस्यैव शमः कारणमुच्यते ॥ 6.3
>
> *āruruksormuneryogaṁ karma kāraṇamucyate*
> *yogārūḍhasya tasyaiva samaḥ kāraṇamucyate*
> —6.3

Simple meaning—For persons receiving training in lokasamgraha, the sustaining factor will be 'commitment to duty.' (i.e. they might not have a complete grasp of the philosophical issues). Persons who have the inner urge to help mankind (and who have fully grasped the philosophical issues too) take up the lokasamgraha-cause 'spontaneously' (because this is part of their nature).

According to the Gita, the expression 'karmayogins' can be used for both these categories of activists. However, in the theory of Spiritual Evolution developed by Sri Aurobindo (reference para 3.16) the spontaneously-inspired karmayogins could be referred to as 'Purna-yogins' (literally meaning 'Yogins who have attained perfection').

4.39. Virtues of peace-promoters. As presented in paras 4.4-4.22, the Gita has looked into the large number of anti-social traits of the peace-breakers. The Gita's depiction of the qualities of peace-promoters is even more detailed. A list of twenty virtues is given in chapter thirteen. A longer list of twenty-six virtues is given in chapter sixteen. Of course, these lists overlap to a large extent. Our present purpose will be served by giving below the list of chapter sixteen:

> अभयं सत्त्वसंशुद्धिर्ज्ञानयोगव्यवस्थितिः ।
> दानं दमश्च यज्ञश्च स्वाध्यायस्तप आर्जवम् ॥
> अहिंसा सत्यमक्रोधस्त्यागः शान्तिरपैशुनम् ।
> दया भूतेष्वलोलुप्त्वं मार्दवं ह्रीरचापलम् ॥
> तेजः क्षमा धृतिः शौचमद्रोहो नातिमानिता ।
> भवन्ति सम्पदं दैवीमभिजातस्य भारत ॥ 16.1-3.

abhayam sattvasaṁśūddhirjñānayogavyavasthitiḥ
dānaṁ damaśca yajñaśca svādhyāyastapa ārjavam
ahiṁsā satyamakrodhastyāgaḥ śāntirapaiśunam
dayā bhūteṣvaloluptvaṁ mārdavaṁ hrīracāpalam
tejaḥ kṣamā dhritiḥ śaucamadroho nātimānitā
bhavanti sampadaṁ daivīmabhijātasya bhārata
—16.1-3

Simple meaning—Qualities of peace-promoters are: fearlessness, purity of mind, wise apportionment of knowledge and applications, sharing, self-control, yajna (sacrifice for lokasamgraha), study of inspiring literature, tapas (self-discipline), uprightness, non-violence, truth, freedom from anger, willingness to give, tranquillity, aversion to fault-finding, compassion to all living beings, freedom from covetousness, gentleness, modesty, absence of fickleness, enthusiasm, forgiveness, fortitude, tolerance, absence of excessive pride.

The main thing to note about these qualities is that they give protective and reformative capability to peace- promoters. For example, protective capability arises from virtues like fearlessness and fortitude. Similarly, reformative capability arises from virtues like non-violence, compassion, tolerance,and forgiveness—the underlying assumption being that peace-promoters will try their best to solve all problems peacefully.

4.40. What additional knowledge? The basis of peace-promotion efforts is the upanisadic knowledge of oneness of all human beings. But practical work of peace-promotion requires not only philosophic knowledge but also other knowledge concerning implementation of the peace process. That is why, chapter thirteen of the Gita has widened the concept of knowledge:

क्षेत्रक्षेत्रज्ञयोर्ज्ञानं
यत्तज्ज्ञानं मतं मम ॥ 13.2

ksetraksetrajnayorjnānaṁ
yattajjnānaṁ mataṁ mama —13.2

Simple meaning—Lord Krishna tells Arjuna, "Complete knowledge means knowledge of Atman (Self) as well as worldly knowledge."

This means that karmayogins working as peace-promoters are advised to have complete knowledge of the problem so as to be able to implement the peace process successfully.

4.41. Role of meditation. In para 3.16, we referred to the meditation-oriented approach to world peace. In contrast thereto, the karmayogin's approach is action-oriented. The difference between the two approaches arises from the different priority that they attach to meditation. Karmayogins believe that the Gita's advice to them, as given, for example, in verse 6.31 (shown below with a slight verbal change) is to use meditation to a limited extent only:

सर्वभूतस्थितं यो मां भजत्येकत्वमास्थितः ।
सर्वथा वर्तमानोऽपि स न योगात् विचाल्यते ॥ 6.31

sarvabhūtasthitaṁ yo māṁ bhajatyekatvamāsthitaḥ
sarvathā vartamānopi sa na yogāt vicālyate —6.31

Simple meaning—Lord Krishna says to Arjuna, "Meditation helps in understanding that the same Atman is in every human being. But life's journey is multi-dimensional. Therefore a karmayogin has to be actively engaged in all the necessary tasks. Only in this way, steadfastness in the yoga of life can be preserved."

4.42. Can monks too be karmayogins, like householders ? It was mentioned in para 4.36 that the main characteristic of karmayogins is their performance of lokasamgraha—activities, without any desire for selfish gains. It is, immaterial, therefore, whether they are householders or monks. The following two verses—the first from the Gita and the second from the Mahabharata—make this clear:

काम्यानां कर्मणां न्यासं
संन्यासं कवयो विदुः ॥ 18.2

त्यागान्न भिक्षुकं विद्यान्न मौढ्यान्न च याचनात् ।
ऋजुस्तु योऽर्थं त्यजति नसुखं विद्धि भिक्षुकम् ॥
–महाभारत 12.18.30

kāmyānāṁ karmaṇāṁ nyāsaṁ
saṁnyāsaṁ kavayo viduḥ —18.2
tygānna bhiksukaṁ vidyānna mauḍhyānna
ca yācanāt
rijustu yorthaṁ tyajati nasukhaṁ viddhi
bhikṣukam —*Mahabharata* 12.18.30

Simple meaning—Monkhood does not mean giving up of all actions, because only the actions prompted by selfish desire need to be given up. (Gita 18.2)

Real monkhood is a state of mind. To leave the home and to take a begging bowl do not signify monkhood. Rather, by giving up attachment, crookedness and selfishness (even if living at home), one is entitled to be regarded as a real monk (Mahabharata 12.18.30).

In practice, most of the karmayogins are householders, but some monks too (like Swami Vivekananda) have been karmayogins.

4.43. Next we move on to karmayoga, the technique of doing work for lokasamgraha. Four main points will show how effective this technique can be, even today:

(i) The technique is efficient for fulfilling the objective to the extent possible.

(ii) It is not counter-productive.

(iii) Although karmayogins put in their best effort, yet the objective may not be fully achieved—even then the karmayogins are not to be blamed.

(iv) The technique is flexible enough to ensure its suitability to different situations.

4.44. Efficiency criterion. The Gita has emphasized this point in many verses out of which two are given below (along with one more which is a condensed version of several of Gita's verses):

योग: कर्मसु कौशलम् ॥ 2.50
कर्मयोगी फलं त्यक्त्वा समाचरति साधनम् ।
तस्मात्तत्कर्म सफलं योग : कर्मसु कौशलम् ॥
अनुद्वेगकरं वाक्यं सत्यं प्रियहितं च यत् ।
स्वाध्यायाभ्यसनं चैव वाङ्मयं तप उच्यते ॥ 17.15

yogaḥ karmasu kauśalam —2.50
karmayogī phalaṁ tyaktvā samācarati sādhanam
tasmāttatkarma saphalaṁ yogaḥ karmasu kauśalam
anudvegakaraṁ vākyaṁ satyaṁ priyahitaṁ ca yat
svādhyāyābhyasanaṁ caiva vānmayaṁ tapa ucyate
—17.15

Simple meaning—The main characteristic of karmayoga is 'efficiency in action'. (2.50)

Two things which contribute to efficiency are: (a) The whole-hearted attention is on the means, and not on the end (although the end is likely to be fine because the means are fine). (b) The means are pure and do not involve violence (because lokasamgraha cannot be attained through violence or suicide).

The efficiency of karmayoga arises also from the fact that, in this technique, harmonious relationships are maintained and the problem in hand is studied thoroughly. (17.15)

4.45. Not counterproductive. There is an in-built check to ensure that the karmayoga technique cannot be counterproductive. In Gita's verse 18.25, five conditions are laid down which must be fulfilled before active work for lokasamgraha is started:

अनुबन्धं क्षयं हिंसामनवेक्ष्य च पौरुषम् ।
मोहादारभ्यते कर्म यत्तत्तामसमुच्यते ॥ 18.25

anubandhaṁ ksayaṁ hiṁsāmanaveksya ca pauruṣam
mohādārabhyate karma yattattāmasamucyate
—18.25

Simple meaning—The five-point check which precedes the start of the lokasamgraha-work by the karmayoga technique is: (a) Will there be any harmful effect of the work? (b) Will any destruction be caused? (c) Will it involve violence or suicide? (d) Is the work feasible, i.e. commensurate with the available resources? (e) Do we have adequate knowledge of the problem?

4.46. No blame to karmayogins. The Gita advises the karmayogins to understand in advance (and to clarify to others too) that, although they will try their best (and will not give up), yet the final outcome is unpredictable. This advice is given in the Gita repeatedly, but we give below only two verses (which are the most famous):

कर्मण्येवाधिकारस्ते मा फलेषु कदाचन ।
मा कर्मफलहेतुर्भूर्मा ते संगोऽस्त्वकर्मणि ॥ 2.47
योगस्थ: कुरु कर्माणि संगं त्यक्त्वा धनञ्जय ।
सिद्ध्यसिद्ध्यो: समो भूत्वा समत्वं योग उच्यते ॥ 2.48

karmanyevādhikāraste mā phaleṣu kadācana
mā karmaphhalaheturbhūrmā te sangostvakarmaṇi
—2.47

yogasthaḥ kuru karmāṇi sangaṁ tyaktvā dhananjaya
siddhyasiddhyoḥ samo bhūtvā samatvaṁ yoga ucyate
—2.48

Simple meaning—Lord Krishna advises Arjuna to put into effect the karmayoga technique, "Your right is limited to making the best effort, but not to expecting any specific outcome. Do not let the outcome be your motive. In any case, do not be an escapist (i.e. do not abandon the effort). Pay whole-hearted attention to the means, and not to the end. If the means are fine, the end is likely to be fine too, but don't lose your mental balance if the end is not fine. The mental state of even-mindedness towards success or failure elevates that action to the status of yoga."

Since these are two of the most famous verses of the Gita, it would be useful to read Mahatma Gandhi's comments on them:

"The Gita says, 'Do your allotted work but renounce its fruit—be detached and work—have no desire for reward, and then work'. This is the unmistakable teaching of the Gita. He who gives up action falls. He who gives up only the reward rises....

"Renunciation of fruit in no way means indifference to the result. In regard to every action, one must know the result that is expected to follow, the means thereto, and the capacity for it. He, who, being thus equipped, is without desire for the result and is yet wholly engrossed in the due fulfilment of the task before him is said to have renounced the fruits of his action....

"Again let no one consider renunciation to mean want of fruit for the renouncer. The Gita reading does not warrant such a meaning. Renunciation means absence of hankering after fruit. As a matter of fact, he who renounces reaps a thousand-fold....

"He who broods over results is like a man given to objects of senses; he is ever distracted, he says goodbye to all scruples, everything is right in his estimation and he therefore resorts to means fair and foul to attain his end ...

"Thinking along these lines, I have felt that in trying to enforce in one's life the central teaching of the Gita, one is bound to follow truth and non-violence."[1]

4.47. Flexibility criterion.This is a special feature of the Gita which introduced dynamism in the field of religion. Not only the concept of karmayoga but also all other concepts involving human relationships, will have to, according to the Gita, be adjusted from time to time, otherwise they will become partly, if not wholly, irrelevant. The following verses from chapters four and seventeen give this message (for an earlier reference to these verses please see para 4.32):

स कालेनेह महता योगो नष्टः परन्तप ॥ 4.2
देशे काले च पात्रे च तद्दानं सात्त्विकं स्मृतम् ॥ 17.20

sa kālenha mahatā yogo naṣṭaḥ parantapa —4.2
deśe kāle ca pātre ca taddānaṁ sāttvikaṁ smritam —17.20

Simple meaning—Whatever religious practice is started, parts of it become irrelevant after a long lapse of time. Therefore, it would be the right decision to make adjustments, in tune with changes in time, place and circumstances.

Applications of Gita's ideas

4.48. At the Parliament of World Religions. As we did in the case of the Upanisads (reference para 3.5), we will start with the Parliament of World Religions held at Chicago in 1893. In his address, Swami Vivekananda quoted three verses from the Gita, to spell out the basis for harmony between different religions:

"The present convention, which is one of the most august assemblies ever held, is in itself a vindication, a declaration to the world of the wonderful doctrine preached in the Gita : "Whoseover worships Me, through whatever path, I accept him; all persons are moving through paths which in the end lead to Me"...

"Unity in diversity is the plan of nature.... In the heart of everything the same truth reigns. The Lord has declared in His incarnation as Krishna, 'I am in every religion as the thread through a string of pearls. Wherever thou seest extraordinary holiness and extraordinary power raising and purifying humanity, know thou that I am there.' "[2]

The three Gita-verses quoted by Swami Vivekananda are given below:

ये यथा मां प्रपद्यन्ते तांस्तथैव भजाम्यहम् ।
मम वर्त्मानुवर्तन्ते मनुष्याः पार्थ सर्वशः ॥ 4.11
मयि सर्वमिदं प्रोतं सूत्रे मणिगणा इव ॥ 7.7
यद्यद् विभूतिमत्सत्त्वं श्रीमदूर्जितमेव वा ।
तत्तदेवावगच्छ त्वं मम तेजोंशसंभवम् ॥ 10.41

ye yathā māṁ prapadyante tāṁstathaiva bhajāmyaham
mama vartmānuvartante manuṣyāḥ pārtha sarvaśaḥ —4.11

mayi sarvamidaṁ protaṁ sūtre maṇigaṇā iva —7.7

yadyad vibhūtimatsattvaṁ śrīmadūrjitameva vā
tattadevāvagaccha tvaṁ mama tejoṁśasambhavam —10.41

Simple meaning—The meaning of the three verses is contained in the address of Swami Vivekananda. (Please also see paras 4.33 and 4.28)

4.49. Motto of Ramakrishna Mission.[3] The second application of the Gita was also made by Swami Vivekananda—this was the establishment of the lokasamgraha-oriented organization, viz. Ramakrishna Mission, in India, in May 1897, with the motto:

आत्मनो मोक्षार्थं जगद्धिताय च

ātmano moksarthaṁ jagaddhitāya ca

Simple meaning—For one's liberation as well as for the good of the world.

This motto is obviously based on the following verse of the Gita (Please also see paras 2.67 and 4.35):

कर्मणैव हि संसिद्धिमास्थिता जनकादयः ।
लोकसंग्रहमेवापि संपश्यन् कर्तुमर्हसि ॥ 3.20
karmaṇaiva hi samsiddhimāsthitā janakādayaḥ
lokasamgrahamevāpi saṁpaśyan kartumarhasi —3.20

Simple meaning—Lord Krishna says to Arjuna, "This message of lokasamgraha which I am giving to you has been exemplified by Janaka and other karmayogins—they attained liberation by working for the good of the world."

4.50. Putting forward the claim for human rights. The third application of the Gita was made by B. G. Tilak (called in India as Lokamanya Tilak) who interpreted this book as an activist, to put forward the claim for human rights (which included Swaraj, political freedom, too). In May 1908, he declared, "Swaraj is my birthright and I will have it."[4] Tilak's approach and the inspiring message that he derived from the Gita, were explained by him through his speeches and books, but we give below a summary in three verses:

कथितं नवरूपेण तेन श्रीकृष्णस्य वचः ।
क्षुद्रं हृदयदौर्बल्यं त्यक्त्वोत्तिष्ठाधिकाराय ॥
जनकार्ये कारावासः तिलकेन प्रतिष्ठितः ।
अलिखत् सः कारावासे गीतारहस्यसद्ग्रन्थम् ॥
गीतासारः कर्मयोगो लोकसंग्रहमूलकः ।
लोकसंग्रहप्राधान्यं लोकमान्येन घोषितम् ॥

kathitaṁ navarūpeṇa tena śrīkrisṇasya vacah
kṣudraṁ hridayadaurbalyaṁ tyaktvottiṣṭhādhikārāya
janakārye kārāvāsaḥ tilakena pratiṣṭhitaḥ
alikhat saḥ kārāvāse gītārahasyasadgrantham
gītāsāraḥ karmayogo lokasaṁgrahamūlakaḥ
lokasaṁgrahaprādhānyaṁ lokamānyena ghoṣitam

Simple meaning—Tilak gave a new interpretation to the Gita. For example, he added the call for human rights to Gita-verse 2.3 which had the message, "Cast off this petty faint-heartedness and arise." It was through his own pioneering example that going to jail as a non-violent freedom fighter began to acquire a special status in people's thinking. For Tilak himself, a long stay in jail became instrumental towards his writing of his most famous book—a Gita commentary entitled "Gitarahasya". In this book, Tilak declared, "Karmayoga is the main teaching of the Gita, and lokasamgraha is the foundation of karmayoga."[5] In India, people called Tilak as "Lokamanya" which means "Revered by the people".

4.51. Aurobindo's support to lokasamgraha. Sri Aurobindo made significant contributions to lokasamgraha, spread over a long time, in the course of which he rose spiritually, from a Karmayogin to Purna-yogin. As a karmayogin, the field of application was the freedom movement in India, and Aurobindo provided strong support to Tilak. In his famous book "Essays on the Gita", Aurobindo highlighted lokasamgraha, and drew special attention to the seven verses of chapter three (i.e. 3.20-26):

"There are few more important passages in the Gita than these seven striking couplets."[6]

As a Purna-yogin, Aurobindo continued to support lokasamgraha, but keeping in mind the changed circumstances, he gave special priority to problems of world peace. In that context, Aurobindo's "Auroville Project" deserves special mention, and we shall do so in the next para.

4.52. Auroville's contribution to world peace. A practical demonstration of how a community might follow Aurobindo's ideals can be seen in the Auroville experiment—a few miles from the Aurobindo Ashram in Pondicherry (India). A four-point Auroville Charter gives an idea of what this 'Cradle of a New World' stands for:

(a) Auroville belongs to nobody in particular. Auroville belongs to humanity as a whole. But to live in Auroville, one must be a willing servitor of the Divine Consciousness.

(b) Auroville will be the place of an unending education, of constant progress and a youth that never ages.

(c) Auroville wants to be the bridge between the past and the future. Taking advantage of all discoveries from without and from within, Auroville will boldly spring towards future realizations.

(d) Auroville will be a site of material and spiritual researches for a living embodiment of an actual Human Unity.[7]

Obviously, Aurobindo's intention was to suggest the establishment of inter-cultural communities like Auroville in different parts of the world (each experiment providing hints as to how newer experiments might serve the cause of world peace more effectively).

4.53. Gandhi's development of non-violent techniques of conflict resolution. Among the many applications of the Gita, made for the promotion of lokasamgraha, the one made by Mahatma Gandhi has attracted world-wide attention, viz. that non-violence is the only, and the best, means through which lokasamgraha can be achieved. On the theoretical front, some scholars have questioned Gandhi's method of picking up non-violence from the Gita, but we support Gandhi's approach. On the practical front, many of the world's leaders (including Dr. Martin Luther King of USA) have confirmed the usefulness of the Gandhian technique and further research is being done all over the world to enhance its applicability to different types of situations. This is a big subject, but here we have no space to write in detail, so we have summarized Gandhi's message in just one verse:

धर्मं चर लोकसंग्रहमूलम् ।
त्यज लोकसंहारं यथाशक्यम् ॥
द्विमंत्राभ्यां प्रेरितो गांधीमतः ।
हिंसावृत्त्या कुतो लोकसंग्रहः ॥

dharmaṁ cara lokasaṁgrahamūlam
tyaja lokasaṁhāraṁ yathāśakyam
dvimantrābhyāṁ prerito gāndhīmataḥ
hiṁsāvrittyā kuto lokasaṁgrahaḥ

Simple meaning—According to Mahatma Gandhi, non-violence is essential for lokasamgraha. How can one hope to bring about the good of the world, asks Gandhi, if one is guided by violence? This can also be expressed in the form of two underlying mantras—guiding principles. First, that we should put into practice only that dharma (religion) which is rooted in lokasamgraha. Secondly, that we should avoid doing, as far as possible, injury or violence to others and also avoid suicide.

4.54. Continuous stream of Gita-inspired NGO's. Following in the footsteps of leaders referred to in the preceding paras, there has been an unabated stream of Gita-inspired lokasamgraha-activists. Madeleine Biardeau made a special study of social service groups in India with a view to identifying their source of inspiration. She writes:

"The term seva, service, is one that recurs quite frequently in the names of many political or social reform groups... Undoubtedly the influence of leaders like Vivekananda lent great credence to the idea of selfless service. It is nevertheless more than likely that all of this took place within pre-existing ideological frames of references, and that the Bhagavad-Gita was its greatest source of inspiration."[8]

Since we have no space here to go into details, we present a summary, in two verses:

> बहवो गीताप्रेरिता निःस्वार्थसेवासंलग्नाः ।
> भूमिहीनान् मत्स्यजनान् साहाय्यकार्यहेतवः ॥
> न सेवा दैन्यभावेन नाहंकारात् मानेच्छया ।
> हरिरूपदरिद्राय मत्वैवं ज्ञानप्रेरिता ॥

> *bahavo gītāpreritā niḥsvārthasevāsaṁlagnāḥ*
> *bhūmihīnān matsyajanān sāhāyyakāryahetavaḥ*
> *na sevā dainyabhāvena nāhaṁkārāt mānecchayā*
> *harirūpadaridrāya matvaivaṁ jñānapreritā*

Simple meaning—There has been a continuous stream of Gita-inspired service-groups. For example, Vinoba Bhave helped landless labores, and Pandurang Shastri helped the poor fishing community. An important characteristic of the service activity taken up by these groups was that it was founded on right knowledge—it viewed service of the poor as service of God—and therefore there was no arrogance, no feeling of superiority, and no desire for any selfish return in the form of honor, etc.

4.55. Secularism strengthened by non-Hindus' reverence for the Gita. Questions relating to secularism were briefly raised in the preceding chapter (reference para 3.15). The suitability of the Gita for strengthening the case for secularism has been stressed by many scholars (including non-Hindu scholars) who wrote books admiring the Gita. Short extracts from two such books are given here. First, P.M. Thomas writes:

"The generosity and the liberality with which the Gita has been interpreted in the twentieth century created a climate for the creation of the secular state in India. It is the religious text which called upon the believers to go beyond sectarian barriers and work for the welfare of the world. Its spirit of toleration provided a theoretical basis for secularism."[9]

Secondly, Donald E. Smith says,

"A theory which has strong roots in the indigenous thought and culture of India, as the lokasamgraha-theory has, is an invaluable asset in creating a deep sense of acceptance of the secular state. Intellectually, psychologically, and religiously, the theory is a powerful one in developing the broad-based conviction that secularism belongs to India."[10]

CHAPTER 5

Elaboration and Extension of Gita's Ideas in the Mahabharata

5.1. Just as the Gita's approach (explained in the preceding chapter) was centered on two new steps, similarly the Mahabharata's approach (or rather the first part of that approach to be presented in this chapter) is also centered on two new steps, outlined in the following two verses (composed by us):

शान्तिभंगः केन कृतो दायित्वं तु द्विपक्षयोः ।
कौरववृत्तिः तामसी दोषः सात्त्विकानामपि ॥
मुख्यतः कर्मयोगिनः चलन्त्यहिंसामार्गेण ।
विशिष्टपरिस्थित्यां तु कुर्वन्ति बलप्रयोगम् ॥

śāntibhangaḥ kena krito dāyitvaṁ tu dvipakṣayoḥ
kauravavrittiḥ tāmasī doṣaḥ sāttvikānāmapi
mukhyataḥ karmayoginaḥ calantyahiṁsāmārgeṇa
viśiṣṭaparisthityāṁ tu kurvanti balaprayogam

Simple meaning—The first new step taken by the Mahabharata is to point out that, although the Kauravas were primarily responsible for the Mahabharata war, the Pandavas too could not be wholly exonerated i.e. could not be declared blameless. In the case of the Kauravas, to be anti-social had become a part of their nature. In the case of the Pandavas, although they were usually peace-loving, yet they committed some mistakes.

The second new step taken by the Mahabharata is to include, in the category of karmayogins, not only those who followed the path of non-violence, but also those who used force under special circumstances. (Of course, in the Mahabharata too, a majority of Karmayogins followed the path of non-violence.)

5.2. Accordingly, the present chapter will consist of three main sections:

(a) Who was responsible for the Mahabharata war?
(b) Extending the concepts of lokasamgraha, karmayogins and karmayoga.
(c) Applications of Mahabharata's ideas.

Who was responsible for the Mahabharata war?

5.3. All the Mahabharata-scholars agree that Duryodhana was primarily responsible for that war, and also that Duhsasana, Sakuni and Karna ganged up with him (to form a gang of four). In the text of the epic itself, Karna, speaking to Lord Krishna, admitted that this gang of four (i.e. Karna himself and three others) was primarily responsible for that war:

योऽयं पृथिव्याः कार्त्स्न्येन विनाशः समुपस्थितः ।
निमित्तं तत्र शकुनिरहं दुःशासनस्तथा ।
दुर्योधनश्च नृपतिर्धृतराष्ट्रसुतोऽभवत् ॥ 5.143.3

yoyaṁ prithivyāḥ kārtsnyena vināśaḥ samupasthitaḥ
nimittaṁ tatra śakuniraham duḥśāsanastathā
duryodhanaśca nripatirdhritarāṣṭrasutobhavat

—5.143.3

Simple meaning—Karna says, O Krishna, everyone knows that the destruction of the entire society that is at hand, has for its cause, four persons, viz. Sakuni, and myself, and Duhsasana, and King Duryodhana.

We have re-arranged Karna's words so as to identify Duryodhana as peace-breaker number one (whom the other three blindly supported):

विघ्नकरो दुर्योधनः तस्यानुजो दुःशासनः ।
शकुनिः द्यूतवंचकः कर्णोऽज्ञानविमोहितः ॥

vighnakaro duryodhanaḥ tasyānujo duḥśāsanaḥ
śakuniḥ dyūtavancakaḥ karṇojñānavimohitaḥ

Simple meaning—Duryodhana was peace-breaker number one. His younger brother Duhsasana blindly supported him. Sakuni was a deceitful gambler, and Karna too supported him, suffering from lack of knowledge as to who his parents are.

Just as, in the preceding chapter, we analysed, on the basis of the Gita, the mental make-up of the peace-breakers (reference paras 4.5-22), similarly we present here a similar analysis pertaining to Duryodhana, Duhsasana, Sakuni, and Karna.

5.4. Considering Duryodhana first, a brief statement was made by Lord Krishna, while addressing Duryodhana's father (i.e. the blind King Dhritarastra):

अशिष्टा गतमर्यादा लोभेन हृतचेतसः ।
धर्मार्थौ पृष्ठतः कृत्वा प्रचरन्ति नृशंसवत् ॥ 5.95.10

aśiṣṭā gatamaryādā lobhena hritacetasaḥ
dharmārthau priṣṭhataḥ kritvā pracaranti
nriśaṁsavat —5.95.10

Simple meaning—Lord Krishna said to Dhritarastra, O King, beware in regard to your son's moral decline. His mental make-up is vitiated by excessive greed, and he has disregarded all norms of civilized conduct. He has set aside righteousness and legitimacy, in his thirst for power, and is now behaving like a cruel person.

A long list of Duryodhana's vices (which are practically unlimited) has been drawn up by Sutton:

"Duryodhana is never mild in his disposition, never gentle in his thoughts, words or deeds, and never forgiving of any offence, real or imagined. He burns with envy over the success of the Pandavas, he is avaricious for power and opulence, and whenever his will is opposed he is consumed by unrestrained wrath. He has no misgivings about the suffering he will cause through waging war. He is vindictive rather than forgiving and has no remorse; he has no real sense of right and wrong and he (with Karna's help) constructs specious arguments that convince no-one in order to justify his misdeeds (Mahabharata 5.21. 9-15). Even after the humiliation of the Pandavas at the dice match, his vindictiveness is such that he wishes to further relish their discomfiture by seeing them suffering in exile in the forest (Mahabharata 3.226).... He shows scant respect for the elders of the family, rejecting the counsel of Gāndhārī, Vidura and others, frequently with a haughty irreverence. He is untruthful and dishonest, as when he lies to his father about the purpose of their journey to Dvaitavana to mock the Pandavas, and his obstinacy is such that he is never seen to alter his resolve in light of superior advice."[1]

5.5. From the above it is clear that seeds of conflict between the Kauravas (headed by Duryodhana) and the Pandavas (headed by Yudhisthira) were sown long ago. However, thirteen years prior to the war, chances of a peaceful settlement appeared to be bright, because Duryodhana agreed that, if the Pandavas spent twelve years in the forest and one year in disguise (without being recognized), then they would get back one-half of the territory. Having fulfilled the conditions stipulated in the thirteen-year-old agreement, the Pandavas wanted their share of the territory. But Duryodhana said "No". Lord Krishna and many other leaders of the community pleaded with Duryodhana to honor the old agreement. In fact, the Pandavas even suggested that they would be satisfied if only five villages were given to them (rather than one-half of the territory). However, all these efforts failed because Duryodhana kept on saying "No":

ध्रियमाणे महाबाहौ मयि सम्प्रति केशव ।
यावद्धि तीक्ष्णया सूच्या विध्येदग्रेण केशव ।
तावदप्यपरित्याज्यं भूमेर्नः पाण्डवान् प्रति ॥ 5.127.25

dhriyamāṇe mahābāhau mayi samprati keśava
yāvaddhi tīkṣṇayā sūcyā vidhyedagreṇa keśava
tāvadapyaparityājyaṁ bhūmernaḥ pāṇḍavān prati
—5.127.25

Simple meaning—Duryodhana's final reply to Lord Krishna's plea for a peaceful settlement was, "So long as I am alive and powerful, I will not give to the Pandavas even that much of territory which could provide space to the point of a sharp needle."

5.6. In the Mahabharata (as in the Gita which is a part of the Mahabharata), Lord Krishna represents peace-promoting elements trying to achieve lokasamgraha (good of the world). Duryodhana as the primary peace-breaker had no soft spot for Krishna. This drawback of Duryodhana is brought out picturesquely in the following narration of the Mahabharata chapter 5.7:

"In order to gather support for their respective causes, representatives of the Kauravas as well as the Pandavas went to Dwarka, the capital city of Krishna's kingdom. Duryodhana (representing the Kauravas) arrived there first. He was admitted to the room where Krishna was taking a nap. There were two chairs for visitors, one near His head and the other near His feet. Duryodhana, out of arrogance, occupied the chair near Krishna's head. Shortly thereafter, Arjuna (representing the Pandavas) arrived, and, out of respect for Krishna, he was glad to occupy the chair near His feet.

"When Krishna got up, He first saw Arjuna and started talking with him. Duryodhana intervened and said that he was the first to arrive there." After listening to both of them, Krishna said, 'I want to help both of you. I shall divide into two parts whatever I have. In part one, I include myself, alone without any army, and with my further declaration that I will not fight. In part two, I include my army, ready to fight. Out of these two options, tell me, Arjuna, what is your preference?'

"Arjuna replied immediately, 'Krishna, I choose you. Whether you fight or not, I want you'."

"Duryodhana felt happy and said , 'I am fully satisfied with the second option, i.e., the army, ready to fight'."

Vaisampayana, the narrator, comments:

कृष्णं चापहृतं ज्ञात्वा सम्प्राप परमां मुदं ।
दुर्योधनस्तु तत् सैन्यं सर्वमादाय पार्थिव : ॥ 5.7.24

krisṇaṁ cāpahritaṁ jñātvā samprāpa paramāṁ mudam
duryodhanastu tat sainyaṁ sarvamādāya pārthivaḥ
—5.7.24

Simple meaning—Duryodhana felt happy because he attached all the importance to the army, and not at all to Krishna's words.

5.7. Peace-breaker number two is Duhsasana, one of the younger brothers of Duryodhana. Duhsasana's attempt to insult Draupadi represents, in a symbolic form, peace-breakers' cruelty against women.The Mahabharata describes in detail how God saved Draupadi from Duhsasana's evil designs, and subsequently during the war, Bhima took revenge and put an end to Duhsasana's life. We give below two verses from the Mahabharata which summarize very briefly both these events:

तदद्भुततमं लोको वीक्ष्य सर्वे महीभृतः ।
शशंसुर्द्रौपदीं तत्र कुत्सन्तो धृतराष्ट्रजम् ॥ 2.68.49
दुःशासने यद् रणे संश्रुतं मे
तद् वै सत्यं कृतमद्येह वीरौ ॥ 8.83.50

tadadbhutatamaṁ loko vīkṣya sarve mahībhritaḥ
śaśaṁsurdraupadīṁ tatra kutsanto dhritarāṣṭrajam
—2.68.49

duḥśāsane yad raṇe saṁśrutaṁ me
tad vai satyaṁ kritamadyeha vīrau —8.83.50

Simple meaning—In that hall (where Duhsasana tried to insult Draupadi but failed to do so because Draupadi was saved by God) every one present was amazed to witness the most extraordinary of all sights—and all of them began to applaud Draupadi and censure Duhsasana.

Subsequently, on the battlefield, Bhima said to Lord Krishna, "I want to inform you that I have taken revenge and put an end to Duhsasana's life (because he had tried to insult Draupadi)."

5.8. Peace-breaker number three is Sakuni, the deceitful gambler who played the game on behalf of Duryodhana. He took advantage of Yudhisthira's weakness for gambling, and gradually won every thing (to the advantage of Duryodhana). At that time, Sakuni felt happy, but the chain of events led to the Mahabharata war, in the course of which Sahadeva (the youngest of the Pandavas) took revenge and put an end to Sakuni's life.We give below two verses from the Mahabharata which summarize very briefly both these events:

सौबलस्त्वभिधायैवं जितकाशी मदोत्कटः ।
जितमित्येव तानक्षान् पुनरेवान्वपद्यत ॥ 2.65.45

तं चापि सर्वे प्रतिपूजयन्तो
दृष्ट्वा ब्रुवाणाः सहदेवमाजौ ।
दिष्ट्या हतो नैकृतिको दुरात्मा
सहात्मजो वीर रणे त्वयेति ॥ 9.28.68

saubalastvabhidhāyaivaṁ jitakāśī madotkaṭaḥ
jitamityeva tānaksān punarevānvapadyata
—2.65.45

taṁ cāpi sarve pratipūjayanto
drisṭvā bruvāṇāḥ sahadevamājau
diṣṭyā hato naikritiko durātmā
sahātmajo vīra raṇe tvayeti —9.28.68

Simple meaning—Sakuni (son of Subala) felt happy to have successfully cheated Yudhisthira in gambling and declared proudly, "I have won".

On the battle-field, all the Pandava-supporters (including Lord Krishna) felt relieved at the death of Sakuni and admiringly spoke to Sahadeva, "You are really a hero to have taken revenge and ended the life of the wicked Sakuni, as well as his son."

5.9. Peace-breaker number four is Karna. Although he was the step-brother of the Pandavas, very few persons (not even Karna) had this knowledge for a long time. Duryodhana gave him a royal title in order to have his support, keeping in mind his extraordinary fighting skill. Thereafter, Karna supported Duryodhana blindly. Upadhyaya has analysed the complicated personality of Karna and explained why he could be viewed as a bundle of four unrighteous elements packed into one:

"Ignorance was the first problem with Karna. For a long time, he did not even know that he was the son of Kunti. Lord Krishna removed this ignorance of Karna, but the latter said that he had already joined hands with Duryodhana and so could not walk into the Pandava-camp."

"Karna's second problem was arrogance. Because of that he picked up a quarrel with Bhisma and declared that, so long as Bhisma was the chief of the Kaurava-camp, he (i.e. Karna) would not actively participate in the war."

"The third problem with Karna was falsehood. He went to Parasurama and became his disciple by telling him a lie (that he i.e. Karna was a Brahmin). But Karna's lie was ultimately detected." Parasurama in his anger pronounced his curse on Karna, 'Since you deceived your guru, the weapon you have learnt shall fail you at the fated moment. You will be unable to recall the mantra when your hour comes.'

"The fourth problem with Karna was 'practising double standard'. He joined the Kauravas in many conspiracies and did not think of abiding by dharma, but during his last battle when he was about to lose, he appealed to Arjuna to observe dharma. Lord Krishna told him that an appeal to dharma can be made only by one who had himself observed it."[2]

We give below one verse from the Mahabharata in which Lord Krishna asked Karna (who appealed for dharma now) why he had not observed dharma (when it was his turn):

यदाभिमन्युं बहवो युद्धे जघ्नुर्महारथाः ।
परिवार्य रणे बालं क्व ते घर्मस्तदा गतः ॥ 8.91.11

yadābhimanyuṁ bahavo yuddhe jaghnurmahārathāḥ
parivārya raṇe bālaṁ kva te dharmastadāgataḥ

—8.91.11

Simple meaning—Lord Krishna asked Karna, "When so many of you jointly surrounded and killed the young hero Abhimanyu, where had your dharma gone?"

5.10. Having looked into the responsibility of the Kauravas for the Mahabharata war, we now draw attention to two mistakes committed by the Pandavas:

> युधिष्ठिरस्य दायित्वं द्यूते रुचिः विनाशिनी ।
> दुर्योधनायोपहासो द्वेषोत्तेजनकारकः ॥
>
> *yudhiṣṭhirasya dāyitvaṁ dyūte ruciḥ vināśinī*
> *duryodhanāyopahāso dveṣottejanakārakah*

Simple meaning—Yudhisthira's big mistake was to participate in gambling. Another mistake of the Pandavas was, they laughed when Duryodhana, dazzled by the craftsmanship of the Pandavas' glamorous palace, mistook a lake to be part of a floor, and fell into it with all his clothes on—this mistake of the Pandavas aggravated the bitterness in Duryodhana's mind.

5.11. Yudhisthira's blunder in regard to gambling was pointed out to him by Lord Krishna:

> आगच्छेयमहं द्यूतं
> बहून् दोषान् प्रदर्शयन् ।
> वीरसेनसुतो यैस्तु
> राज्यात् प्रभ्रंशितः पुरा ॥ 3.13.2,5
>
> *āgaccheyamahaṁ dyūtaṁ*
> *bahūn doṣān pradarśayan*
> *vīrasenasuto yaistu*
> *rājyāt prabhraṁśitaḥ purā* —3.13.2,5

Simple meaning—Lord Krishna said to Yudhisthira , "I wish I had come to the hall where gambling took place. Then I would have told everyone about the great destruction that gambling causes, giving the example of King Nala who lost his kingdom due to gambling."

5.12. In regard to the mistaken laughter of the Pandavas at Duryodhana's humiliation, the Mahabharata—text blames Bhima (and not Draupadi, although she is often blamed):

वापीं मत्वा स्थलमिव सवासा: प्रापतज्जले ।
जले निपतितं दृष्ट्वा भीमसेनो महाबलः ।
जहास जहसुश्चैव किंकराश्च सुयोधनम् ॥ 2.47.7

vāpīm̐ matvā sthalamiva savāsāḥ prāpatajjale
jale nipatitam̐ driṣṭvā bhīmaseno mahābalaḥ
jahāsa jahasuścaiva kinkarāśca suyodhanam
—2.47.7

Simple meaning—Duryodhana mistook a lake as part of a floor and fell into it with all his clothes on. Seeing this, Bhima laughed, and the attendants too laughed.

5.13. Having looked into the two mistakes of the Pandavas, we examine the role of Drona. The Mahabharata—text indirectly blames Drona for not giving peace-oriented education to the Kauravas. Bhisma, while appointing Drona, had checked mainly the arms-related skills of the latter and had ignored his spirituality-related shortcomings. Although Drona was the guru of the Kauravas and Pandavas, he gave preferential treatment to his own son Ashwatthama, and the son too (after growing up) acted unrighteously (murdering Draupadi's sons while they were asleep) and Shirmad-Bhagavata says that Draupadi still pardoned Ashwatthama. We summarize Drona's role in the following two verses:

कौरववृत्ति: तामसी दायित्वं गुरूणामपि ।
सात्त्विकमूल्यवर्धका न दत्ता शिक्षा द्रोणेन ॥
गुरुरूपेण द्रोणेन न प्राप्ता पूर्णत्वस्थिति: ।
अन्याय एकलव्याय द्वेषभावो द्रुपदाय ॥

kauravavrittiḥ tāmasī dāyitvam̐ gurūṇāmapi
sāttvikamūlyavardhakā na dattā śiksā droṇena
gururūpeṇa droṇena na prāptāḥ pūrṇatvasthitiḥ
anyāya ekalavyāya dveṣabhāvo drupadāya

Simple meaning—The Kauravas have been blamed for being anti-social, but their teacher Drona too can be assigned a part of the blame because he did not give them the right education.

Drona's spirituality-related shortcomings were exemplified by his unjust behaviour towards Ekalavya and his animosity towards Drupada.

5.14. Since Bhisma had taken the decision to appoint Drona, a part of the blame can be assigned to Bhisma too. Another blameworthy decision taken by Bhisma, in the early part of the Mahabharata, was the abduction of three young women from Varanasi, in order to get them married to Vichitravirya—one of these women (Amba) protested to Bhisma and was allowed to leave (but filled with bitterness), and Bhisma himself predicted that he will suffer defeat on the battlefield because of Amba. We summarize Bhisma's mistakes (which are narrated in different parts of the Mahabharata) in the following verse:

आदौ तु श्रीभीष्मेणापि कृतमनुचितं कर्म ।
अम्बापहरणं तथा नियुक्तिः गुरुद्रोणस्य ॥

ādau tu śrībhīṣmeṇāpi kritamanucitaṁ karma
ambāpaharaṇaṁ tathā niyuktiḥ gurudroṇasya

Simple meaning—Even Bhisma committed mistakes in the early part of the Mahabharata, for example, abduction of Amba, and appointment of Drona as guru.

Elaborating and extending concepts of lokasamgraha, karmayogins and karmayoga

5.15. First, we present selected verses of the Mahabharata which support and elaborate Gita's formulation of these concepts, as given in paras 4.23-47, and thereafter we shall indicate the extensions made by the Mahabharata. The sequence of presentation will be the same as in the preceding chapter (i.e. we start with lokasamgraha and then move on to karmayogins and karmayoga).

5.16. The Gita gave the message of lokasamgraha from ten angles, and we shall give Mahabharata verses relating to each of them.

Lokasamgraha in the context of Vedic yajna. The Gita re-defined the Vedic yajna as acts of social service, in the light of which it is not necessary to light fire and make offerings to God through the fire. The Mahabharata added that even if some one still wanted to perform yajna in the Vedic style, the minimum condition for that should be to desist from making animal sacrifice:

कामकाराद् विहिंसन्ति बहिर्वेद्यां पशून् नराः ।
धूर्तैः प्रवर्तितं ह्येतन्नैतद् वेदेषु कल्पितम् ॥12.265.5,9

kāmakārād vihiṁsanti bahirvedyāṁ paśūn narāḥ
dhūrtaiḥ pravartitaṁ hyetannaitad vedeṣu kalpitam
—12.265. 5,9

Simple meaning—Those who sacrifice animals in any yajna, are ignorant and mischievous persons, who have misinterpreted the Vedas in order to satisfy their own desire to eat meat.

5.17. Extending Kaṭha Upanisad. The Gita extended the Upanisadic concept of Sreyas to lokasamgraha (helping one another). The Mahabharata confirmed the Gita's approach by means of the following story:

Although life-breath is essentially a unified entity, yoga-experts have identified five variations of this entity and named them as prana, apana, udana, samana, and vyana. These five, instead of realizing their essential unity, adopted a competitive attitude, each one vying for superiority, but they left the decision (regarding who is superior) to the creator (Brahma). The decision announced by Brahma is summarized in the following verse:

सर्वे स्वविषये श्रेष्ठा : सर्वे चान्योन्यधर्मिणः ।
परस्परस्य सुहृदो भावयन्तः परस्परम् ।
स्वस्ति व्रजत भद्रं वो धारयध्वं परस्परम् ॥ 14.23.24

sarve svaviṣaye śreṣṭhāḥ sarve cānyonyadharmiṇaḥ
parasparasya suhrido bhāvayantaḥ parasparam
svasti vrajata bhadraṁ vo dhārayadhvaṁ parasparam
—14.23.24

Simple meaning—Each of you is great in your own sphere, but the greatness of each depends also upon the support received from others. Therefore, be friends of one another and help one another. All of you will certainly prosper if you uphold one another.

5.18. Lokasamgraha as repayment of debt. The Gita advised everyone that, since human capabilities are developed with the support of the society, the debt to society should be voluntarily repaid by helping all the members of the society to the best of one's ability. The Mahabharata added that the debt to society is qualitatively different from a bank-loan:

देवतातिथिभूतेभ्यः पितृभ्यश्चात्मनस्तथा ।
ऋणवान् जायते मर्त्यस्तस्मादनृणतां व्रजेत् ॥ 12.292.9
ऋणवन्तः सदा मर्त्याः ॥ 12.269.16

devatātithibhūtebhyaḥ pitribhyaścātmanastathā
riṇavān jāyate martyastasmādanriṇatāṁ vrajet
—2.292.9
riṇavantaḥ sadā martyāḥ —12.269.16

Simple meaning—Everyone should realize that, all the time from one's birth onward, one takes help from five main sources and therefore one is indebted to them—these sources being gods (or god-like beings like parents and teachers), guests, all beings, ancestors, and one's own Atman (which is the same as Brahman or God). One must try to do those things in one's life which can be considered as discharging (or repaying) one's debt. Furthermore, it is clear that the debt to society can never be fully repaid.

5.19. Lokasaṁgraha linked to sympathy and philosophic equality. The Gita stressed the importance of combining philosophic equality and sympathy. The Mahabharata added that such a combination is particularly important when we deal with the weaker section of the society:

प्रत्याख्याने च दाने च सुखदुःखे प्रियाप्रिये ।
आत्मौपम्येन पुरुषः प्रमाणमधिगच्छति ॥ 13.113.9
त्रस्तं च व्याधितं कृशं नित्यमाश्वासयन्ति ते ॥ 12.228.41

pratyākhyāne ca dāne ca sukhaduḥkhe priyāpriye
ātmaupamyena puruṣaḥ pramāṇamadhigacchati
—13.113.9

trastaṁ ca vyādhitaṁ kriśaṁ nityamāśvāsayanti te
—12.228.41

Simple meaning—The philosophic concept of atmaupamya means seeing the same Atman in all the beings. When this is combined with sympathy, we get the following yardstick for behaviour—just as we feel happy to receive a pleasant thing, and we feel unhappy in the opposite situation, every one else will feel the same way, therefore we act accordingly, particularly when we deal with those who are oppressed, weak and disabled.

5.20. Lokasamgraha as a corrective to group loyalty. The Gita's message was that, if there is a conflict between group loyalty and good of all, then group loyalty must have a lower priority than good of all, particularly if group loyalty is accompanied with hatred towards other people. If Duryodhana had accepted this message, then there would have been no Mahabharata war. Since Duryodhana did not even want to listen, Vidura tried to convince Dhritarastra (i.e. Duryodhana's father):

त्यजेत् कुलार्थे पुरुषं ग्रामस्यार्थे कुलं त्यजेत् ।
ग्रामं जनपदस्यार्थे आत्मार्थे पृथिवीं त्यजेत् ॥ 5.37.17

सुलभाः पुरुषा राजन् सततं प्रियवादिनः ।
अप्रियस्य तु पथ्यस्य वक्ता श्रोता च दुर्लभः ॥ 5.37.15

tyajet kulārthe puruṣaṁ grāmasyārthe kulaṁ tyajet
grāmaṁ janapadasyārthe ātmārthe prithivīṁ tyajet
—5.37.17

sulabhāḥ puruṣā rājan satataṁ priyavādinaḥ
apriyasya tu pathyasya vaktā śrotā ca durlabhaḥ
—5.37.15

Simple meaning—Vidura said to Dhritarastra, "O King, it is better to give up one person (i.e. Duryodhana) for the sake of the family, similarly, give up the family for the village, and the village for the state. For the sake of Atman (i.e. truth and high principles), even the state could be given up." 5.37.17.

Vidura further pleaded, "O King, most of your advisers tell you what will please you, but I am your genuine well-wisher, therefore I have told you what will do good to you, even if it may not please you. Not many people want to hear such advice and therefore, not many people would dare give such advice. In this crisis situation, I have taken the courage to say these words and I hope you will listen to me and do what will do good to all." 5.37.15

5.21. Lokasamgraha as a healer of fragmentation wounds. The Gita expressed the hope that, since the philosophy of separateness is the root cause of destruction, arrangements will be made to give right education to peace-breakers as well as to would be peace-breakers, to heal the wounds of fragmentation. The Mahabharata repeated Gita's hope, but stressed the need for redoubled effort in the field of education because of the double jump involved in rising from Tamas to Sattva (through the intermediary stage of Rajas):

यदा भूतपृथग्भावमेकस्थमनुपश्यति ।
तत एव च विस्तारं ब्रह्म सम्पद्यते तदा ॥ 12.17.23
ज्ञानादपेत्य या वृत्तिः सा विनाशयति सदा ।
ज्ञानं प्लावयते सर्वं यो ज्ञानं ह्ययनुवर्तते ॥ 12.269.50
तामसस्याधमं स्थानं राजसस्येह मध्यमम् ।
सात्त्विकस्योत्तमं स्थानं प्राहुरध्यात्मचिन्तकाः ॥ 12.314.3

yadā bhūtaprithagbhāvamekasthamanupaśyati
tata eva ca vistāraṁ brahma sampadyate tadā
—12.17.23
jnānādapetya yā vrittiḥ sā vināśayati sadā
jñānaṁ plāvayate sarvaṁ yo jnānaṁ hyanuvartate
—12.269.50
tāmasasyādhamaṁ sthānaṁ rājasasyeha madhyamam
sāttvikasyottamaṁ sthānaṁ prāhuradhyātmacintakāḥ
—12.314.3

Simple meaning—The root cause of destruction is lack of right knowledge i.e. the philosophy of separateness. Peace can be established by the acquisition of right knowledge i.e. the philosophy of oneness of all human beings. Destruction is the lowest state of Tamas, one step higher (peace-maintenance) is the state of Rajas, and peace-promotion is the highest state of Sattva. Since we want to move up from destruction to peace-promotion, it involves a two-step rise for which we need re-doubled effort in the field of education.

5.22. Lokasamgraha as a catalyst for transforming values. The Gita suggested a radical transformation of the value system of the society so as to give the highest priority to world peace. The Mahabharata strengthened this suggestion further by adding that, if any of our friends breaks peace, then we should plead with that person, politely but firmly, to discontinue anti-social activities (which will have no place in the transformed value system):

सर्वतश्च प्रशान्ता ये सर्वभूतहिते रताः ।
न क्रुद्ध्यन्ति न निन्दन्ति नापराध्यन्ति कर्हिचित् ॥ 12.229.15
न हिंस्यात् सर्वभूतानि मैत्रायणगतश्चरेत् ॥ 12.278.5
स्निग्धैश्च क्रियमाणानि कर्माणीह निवर्तयेत् ।
हिंसात्मकानि सर्वाणि प्रियवादेन सर्वदा ॥ 12.297.9

sarvataśca praśāntā ye sarvabhūtahite ratāḥ
na kruddhyanti na nindanti nāparādhyanti karhicit
—12.229.15

na hiṁsyāt sarvabhūtāni maitrāyaṇagataścaret
—12.278.5

snigdhaiśca kriyamāṇāni karmāṇīha nivartayet
hiṁsātmakāni sarvāṇi priyavādena sarvadā
—12. 297.9

Simple meaning—In the transformed value system, the highest priority will be given to peace, both internal and external. This will be accompanied with mutual friendliness and the desire to help one another, care being taken to avoid anger as well as the tendency to blame one another or to harm one another. In addition to all these, corrective action will be taken by the people,viz. to put pressure, politely, on any friend who might deviate from the path of peace.

5.23. Lokasamgraha interlinked with pluralistic society. The Gita put forward the principle of freedom of choice that every member of the society has in regard to one's religious belief, which is the basis of a pluralistic society. In order to strengthen this principle, the Mahabharata explained that the word 'dharma' is essentially centered on social harmony, and not on religious belief which is a matter of individual choice:

धारणाद् धर्ममित्याहुर्धर्मो धारयते प्रजा: ।
यत् स्याद् धारणसंयुक्तं स धर्म इति निश्चय: ॥ 8.68.58
बहुद्वारस्य धर्मस्य ॥ 12.174.2

dhāraṇād dharmamityāhurdharmo dhārayate prajāḥ
yat syād dhāraṇasaṁyuktaṁ sa dharma iti niścayaḥ
—8.68.58

bahudvārasya dharmasya —12.174.2

Simple meaning—The main characteristic of dharma is the keeping together of the society, and not the specification of any particular religious belief. In other words, the principles and practices that hold the society together, constitute dharma. Since every member of the society can freely choose one's religious belief, it is obvious that "dharma has many doors" i.e. there is no restriction on people's choices.

5.24. Lokasamgraha as participation in God's work. The Gita declared that God is constantly watching whether the world and all its citizens are safe, sound and happy, and therefore, whosoever amongst the human beings is voluntarily engaged in lokasamgraha-activities, is participating in God's work. The Mahabharata has described how the demon Vritrasur, after seeing God, gave up destructive activities and became a peace-promoter. (Vritrasura's message of peace is called "Vritra-Gita" i.e. declared by the Mahabharata to be worthy of great honor).

In this way, the Mahabharata gives a clear message that, whosoever is trying to bring about world peace, is participating in God's work:

यदा मे भगवान् दृष्टो हरिर्नारायणः प्रभुः । 12.279.28
तदा भूत्वा विकल्मषः तथैव भूत्वा विपाप्मा ॥ 12.280.57

yadā me bhagavān dristo harirnārāyanaḥ prabhuḥ
—12.279.28
tadā bhūtvā vikalmaṣaḥ tathaiva bhūtvā vipāpmā
—12.280.57

Simple meaning—Shukracharya asked Vritrasura, "How is it that you have changed, from a peace-breaker to a peace-promoter?" Vritrasura replied, "When I saw Narayana (God), I became free from all my sins i.e. peace-breaking tendencies."

5.25. Lokasamgraha as exemplified by Karmayogins. In order to clarify further what lokasamgraha means, the Gita gives the example of the famous King Janaka of ancient India. The Mahabharata has many such examples. In fact, Janaka's example too was completed (in para 4.35) with the help of the Mahabharata. Here it will be enough if we give one more example from the Mahabharata, and we do so by quoting the following verse about another famous king of ancient India, viz. Asvapati:

आसीन्मद्रेषु धर्मात्मा राजा परमधार्मिकः ।
पार्थिवोऽश्वपतिर्नाम सर्वभूतहिते रतः ॥ 3.293.5

āsīnmadreṣu dharmātmā rājā paramadhārmikaḥ
pārthivośvapatirnāma sarvabhūtahite rataḥ
—3.293.5

Simple meaning—Once upon a time, long ago, Asvapati was the King of Madra-desa. His devotion to dharma was perfect. He was always engaged in doing good to all the people.

5.26. Extension by the Mahabharata to the eleventh angle. Having given examples of Mahabharata's support to Gita's concept of lokasamgraha, from all the ten angles, we now draw attention to the eleventh angle (viz. environmental angle) which is implicit in the Gita, but has been made explicit in the Mahabharata:

> वनस्पतीन् भक्ष्यफलान्
> न च्छिन्द्युर्विषये तव ॥ 12.89.1
>
> *vanaspatīn bhaksyaphalān*
> *na cchindyurviṣaye tava* —12.89.1

Simple meaning—Bhisma gave specific advice to Yudhisthira, "As a king you should ensure that plants and trees which yield edible fruits should not be cut down in your kingdom."

5.27. Presentation on karmayogins. Having completed the presentation on lokasamgraha, we now move on to karmayogins. In this context too, we shall first indicate how the Mahabharata has elaborated Gita's ideas. For example, the Gita has envisaged that karmayogins could be any of the normal human beings (i.e. male or female, and similarly not subject to any other restriction). The Mahabharata has given many examples of karmayogins, to substantiate Gita's statement, particularly in two directions:

(a) Karmayogins need not be kings or persons belonging only to the privileged section of the society.

(b) The number of women, among karmayogins, is not negligible.

5.28. Diversification of karmayogins. One of the most famous karmayogins, described in detail in the Mahabharata, is a butcher. His message has been honored as "Vyadha-Gita". (Please see para 5.34) Another famous karmayogin is an ordinary trader (Tuladhara by name). (Please see para 7.14). The list of karmayogins in the Mahabharata also includes a Naga couple (Padmanabha and his wife).

5.29. Women karmayogins. The Mahabharata has paid tribute to an ordinary (un-named) housewife who proved to be a great karmayogin. (Please see para 5.34). While admiring both Janaka and his wife as karmayogins, the Mahabharata has depicted the wife's role to be as important as that of Janaka. Savitri, the daughter of the famous king Asvapati, attained fame as a great karmayogin. (Please see para 6.22)

5.30. Extension by the Mahabharata. An important characteristic of karmayogins, according to the Gita, is that they are assumed to try their best to solve all problems peacefully. Although this applies to most of the karmayogins listed in the Mahabharata too, yet the Mahabharata has also honored Kartikeya (also known as Skanda or Kumar) who had to use force to overpower the peace-breakers:

षड्वक्त्रस्य कुमारस्य कर्म लोकहिताय वै ॥ 3.226.15
सैनापत्येनाभिषिक्तो हन्तुं महिषासुरं च ॥ 3.231.28

ṣaḍvaktrasya kumārasya karma lokahitāya vai
—3. 226.15
saināpatyenābhiṣikto hantuṁ mahiṣāsuraṁ ca
—3.231.28

Simple meaning—Kartikeya (Kumar) was appointed commander-in-chief so that the fierce demon Mahisasura could be overpowered, to save the world from destruction.

5.31. Mahabharata's elaboration of the theory of karmayoga. Gita's concept of karmayoga has been elaborated in the Mahabharata (not covering all the ideas in one place, but rather in parts) through a large number of narrations, of which the most important are the following (this list does not include Bhagavad-Gita):

(a) Anu-Gita
(b) Vyadha-Gita
(c) Story of Tuladhara and Jajali
(d) Dialogue between Yudhisthira and Yaksa
(e) Narayaniya Dharma
(f) Ten more Gita's (viz. Pingala-Gita, Sampaka-Gita, Manki-Gita, Bodhya-Gita, Vichakhnu-Gita, Harita-Gita, Vritra-Gita, Parasara-Gita, Hamsa-Gita, Kama-Gita).

All of these are interesting narrations, but we have no space here to write about them.[3]

5.32. Mahabharata's modification in the theory of karmayoga. One of the assumptions of the theory of karmayoga, as formulated by the Gita, is that lokasamgraha (good of all) includes the good of the individual. The Mahabharata has, however, considered the rare possibility that there might be a clash between these two. Through a dialogue between Lord Krishna and Arjuna (which is in a different part of the Mahabharata i.e. different from the narrations listed in the preceding para), a story of Kausika is told, the message thereof being that, if there is a clash between lokasamgraha and the good of the individual, then lokasamgraha deserves priority. This story is summarized in the next para.

5.33. Story of Kausika. Lord Krishna tells this story to Arjuna.

कौशिकोऽप्यभवद् विप्रस्तपस्वी नो बहुश्रुतः ।
नदीनां संगमे ग्रमाददूरात् स किलावसत् ॥ 8.69.46

kauśikopyabhavad viprastapasvī no bahuśrutaḥ
nadīnāṁ sangame grāmādadūrāt sa kilāvasat
—8.69.46

Simple meaning—A brahmin named Kausika was an expert in austerities (tapas), but had no real knowledge of scriptures. He lived near a junction of roads, not far from the village.

सत्यं मया सदा वाच्यमिति तस्याभवद् व्रतम् ।
सत्यवादीति विख्यातः स तदाऽसीद् धनंजय ॥ 8.69.47

satyaṁ mayā sadā vācyamiti tasyābhavad vratam
satyavādīti vikhyātaḥ sa tadāsīd dhananjaya
—8.69.47

Simple meaning—Kausika took a vow that he will always speak the truth. After a while, he became known as a 'teller of truth'.

अथ दस्युभयात् केचित् तदा तद् वनमाविशन् ।
तत्रापि दस्यवः क्रुद्धास्तानमार्गन्त यत्नतः ॥ 8.69.48

atha dasyubhayāt kecit tadā tad vanamāviśan
tatrāpi dasyavaḥ kruddhāstānamārgantah yatnataḥ
—8.69.48

Simple meaning—One day, some innocent persons, trying to escape from dacoits, hid themselves in a wooded area near that road-junction. Shortly after that, the dacoits too arrived at that junction.

अथ कौशिकमभ्येत्य प्राहुस्ते सत्यवादिनम् ।
कतमेन पथा याता भगवन् बहवो जनाः ॥ 8.69.49
सत्येन पृष्टः प्रब्रूहि यदि तान् वेत्थ शंस नः । 8.69.50

atha kauśikamabhyetya prāhuste satyavādinam
katamena pathā yātā bhagavan bahavo janāḥ
—8.69.49
satyena priṣṭaḥ prabrūhi yadi tān vettha śaṁsa naḥ
—8.69.50

Simple meaning—The dacoits asked Kausika, "We are in pursuit of some persons but they escaped in this direction. You are known as a truth-teller. Please tell us where we can catch hold of them."

स पृष्टः कौशिकः सत्यं वचनं तानुवाच ह ॥ 8.69.50
बहुवृक्षलतागुल्ममेतद् वनमुपाश्रिताः ।
इति तान् ख्यापयामास तेभ्यस्तत्त्वं स कौशिकः ॥ 8.69.51

sa priṣṭaḥ kauśikaḥ satyaṁ vacanaṁ tānuvāca ha
—8.69.50
bahuvriksalatāgulmametad vanamupāsritāḥ
iti tān khyāpayāmāsa tebhyaśtattvaṁ sa kauśikaḥ
—8.69.51

Simple meaning—It was clear to Kausika that dacoits are in pursuit of innocent persons, still he, instead of protecting innocent persons, helped the dacoits by giving them all the information.

ततस्ते तान् समासाद्य क्रूरा जघ्नुरिति श्रुतिः ।
तेनाधर्मेण महता वाग्दुरुक्तेन कौशिकः ॥ 8.69.52

tataste tān samāsādya krūrā jaghnuriti śrutiḥ
tenādharmeṇa mahatā vāgduruktena kauśikaḥ
—8.69.52

Simple meaning—With the help of the information received from Kausika, the dacoits caught hold of the innocent persons, robbed them and killed them. In fact, Kausika was responsible for this tragedy because his reply to the dacoits, although technically correct, was completely wrong.

येऽन्यायेन जिहीर्षन्तो धर्ममिच्छन्ति कर्हिचित् ।
अकूजनेन मोक्षं वा नानुकूजेत् कथंचन ॥ 8.69.59

yenyāyena jihīrṣanto dharmamicchanti karhicit
akūjanena mokṣaṁ vā nānukūjet kathancana
—8.69.59

Simple meaning—O Arjuna, in a situation like this, when telling the truth will only help anti-social people, then it is best not to give any information at all.

अवश्यं कूजितव्ये वा शंकेरन्नप्यकूजतः ।
श्रेयस्तत्रानृतं वक्तुं तत् सत्यमविचारितम् ॥ 8.69.60

avaśyaṁ kūjitavye vā śankarannapyakūjataḥ
śreyastatrānritaṁ vaktuṁ tat satyamavicāritam
—8.69.60

Simple meaning—Lord Krishna concluded Kausika's story by saying, "However, if giving no information at all is likely to create suspicion, then it becomes inevitable to give some information (right or wrong). My advice is that telling untruth under such circumstances is to be considered as telling the truth."

Arvind Sharma, after analysing Kausika's story, expresses the following view:

"This story was narrated to Arjuna by Krishna as a warning against a purely formal approach to ethics. I would like to use it here to illustrate the point how general good (lokasamgraha) may require the sacrifice of personal morality, narrowly conceived."[4]

Applications of Mahabharata's ideas

5.34. Vivekananda's glorification of karmayogins from the underprivileged section of society. Swami Vivekananda, after speaking at the Parliament of World Religions at Chicago in 1893, addressed many gatherings in USA where he glorified the Mahabharata for having identified famous karmayogins belonging to the underprivileged section of the society. He included a summary of some of these speeches in his book entitled "Karma Yoga". We present here an extract from this book:

"A young Sannyasin developed yogic power, and when he angrily looked at a crow, he noticed that the crow was burnt to ashes. Conscious of his new power, he went to a house nearby to beg for food. The housewife was busy nursing her sick husband, so she asked the Sannyasin to wait. The Sannyasin retorted, 'Do you have any idea how much yogic power I have?' The housewife replied, 'Sorry that you had to wait, dear Yogin, but I am not a crow.' The Sannyasin cooled down and asked, 'How do you know about the crow?' The housewife said, 'I suggest you go to Mithila and see the butcher there, he will answer your question.'

"When the Sannyasin reached Mithila, he saw from a distance, a big fat butcher selling meat. The Sannyasin thought, 'Is this the man to answer my question? He is the incarnation of a demon, if he is anything.' Just then the butcher came forward and asked the Sannyasin, 'Are you the Yogin whom that lady sent to me?'

"The Sannyasin was wonder-struck. But he sat down like a disciple and requested the butcher to teach him about dharma. The Mahabharata has glorified the teachings of the butcher, by calling it Vyādha-Gita."[5]

5.35. Mahabharata as the key to clarify Gandhi's difference from Tilak.To achieve the independence of India from the British rule, B.G. Tilak, a prominent leader of the Congress Party, suggested in 1897 that the freedom struggle should be guided by the Gita. At that time, M.K. Gandhi was in South Africa and he too used the Gita to guide the struggle against racial discrimination, but he insisted that the struggle would be perfectly non-violent. Gandhi, after achieving success in South Africa by non-violent means, returned to India in 1915. During 1919, when Tilak's failing health restricted his movements, the Congress Party approached Gandhi to take over the leadership of the freedom struggle. Gandhi agreed but specified the condition that the Party will have to declare its whole-hearted support to non-violence. Upto that point, Tilak's policy was 'peacefully if possible, but otherwise by force'. At a decision-making gathering of the Party, a majority of delegates supported Gandhi. After Tilak's death in 1920, his supporters too joined the mainstream led by Gandhi. However, the difference between the two interpretations of the Gita—one by Tilak, and another by Gandhi—has since become an important academic issue, needing clarification as to what caused it. It can now be stated that the Mahabharata holds the key to clarify the issue. Since Tilak considered the Gita to be an integral part of the Mahabharata, his approach was obviously influenced by the Mahabharata. On the other hand, since Gandhi interpreted the Gita, by itself, i.e. without allowing the Mahabharata to influence his approach, he ruled out the use of force at any stage.

5.36. Suggestion to replace dictatorial governments by democracies. In the Mahabharata, Duryodhana was primarily responsible for the war because he kept on saying "No" to every suggestion for peace. If this event is analysed through the terminology of the twenty-first century, it can be stated that peace efforts failed because Duryodhana was a dictator. If Duryodhana had been an elected head of a democratic form of Government, then he could not have ignored the advice of leaders like Bhisma, Vidura and Drona. In other words, United Nations can draw a lesson from the Mahabharata and take necessary action to replace dictatorial governments by democracies, in the interest of world peace. Of course, the cooperation of the concerned governments will be needed, for a peaceful change, from dictatorship to democracy.

5.37. Suggestion for making the peace process a mass movement. The Mahabharata has given several examples of karmayogins who belonged to different sections of the society. In today's world, it means that peace-promoters could belong to any section of the society. United Nations can draw a lesson from this and try to make the peace process a mass movement, so that all the people of the world can make their contribution. This point will be discussed in detail in chapter eight. (Please see para 8.28)

CHAPTER 6

Mahabharata's Messages of Peace for Consideration by Governments

6.1. The preceding chapter presented some of the Mahabharata's messages of peace. However, those messages constitute only one-fourth of what we will take from the Mahabharata, for inclusion in the whole of this book. In fact, the Mahabharata has a vast ocean-like coverage, as is clear from its own declaration:

धर्मे चार्थे च कामे च मोक्षे च भरतर्षभ ।
यदिहास्ति तदन्यत्र यन्नेहास्ति न कुत्रचित् ॥ 18.5.50

dharme cārthe ca kāme ca mokse ca bharatarṣabha
yadihāsti tadanyatra yannehāsti na kutracit

—18.5.50

Simple meaning—Vaisampayana declared in the last chapter of the Mahabharata, "On the topics of dharma, artha, kama and moksa (i.e. the four goals of life), what you find in this book may be found elsewhere, but whatever is not found here, you will not be able to find anywhere else."

6.2. Out of all the Parva's (sections) of the Mahabharata, the most important for our present purpose is Shanti Parva (the title itself means 'Parva focusing on peace'). Background information about this Parva will be given in the following paras which will also set the stage for obtaining therefrom the long series of messages of peace. In the present chapter, we will summarize only one-third of Shanti-Parva. Following the pattern of the preceding chapter, this chapter too will consist of three main sections:

(a) Shanti-Parva, the principal source for messages of peace
(b) Main messages given to Yudhisthira in the first one-third of Shanti-Parva (i.e. Raja-dharma).
(c) Potential applications of these messages in the context of the twenty-first century.

Shanti-Parva, the principal source for messages of peace

6.3. Out of a total of eighteen Parva's of the Mahabharata, Shanti-Parva occurs at number twelve. The great Kaurava leader, Bhisma had fallen down on the battlefield in Parva number six, but he did not die because he had the yogic power to determine the exact timing of his passing away. The war ended in Parva number nine. After the war was over, although Yudhisthira was the winner, he felt unhappy that so many lives of near and dear ones were lost. He then received advice from several great personalities of the Mahabharata, but the longest dialogue took place between Yudhisthira and Bhisma. That dialogue is narrated in Shanti-Parva (and it spills over to the next Parva viz. Anusasana Parva too).

6.4. Shanti-Parva is the longest parva in the Mahabharata, and when combined with Anusasana Parva, accounts for more than one-fourth of the entire epic. Shanti-Parva by itself has three distinct parts:

(i) Raja-dharma
(i) Apad-dharma
(iii) Moksa-dharma

From the first part, i.e. Raja-dharma, we will derive, in the present chapter, messages as to what governments can do to establish world peace. From the third part (a change of order is appropriate to our purpose), we will derive, in the next chapter, messages as to what religious leaders can do to establish world peace. Finally, from the second part, i.e. Apad-dharma,we will derive, in the eighth chapter, messages as to what all others can do to establish world peace because Apad-dharma signifies action to be taken when there is an emergency. Whenever these messages, to be derived from Shanti-Parva, will need to be strengthened with the help of other Parva's of the Mahabharata, we will freely do so. Furthermore, we will not look at the three parts of Shanti-Parva as water-tight compartments because they re-inforce one another.

6.5. Within Raja-dharma itself (which is the focus of our attention now), the contents of the opening chapter are considered particularly significant by Mahatma Gandhi. Yudhisthira is depicted there, not in a joyous mood of celebration of victory in the war, but rather in a state of shock and repentance:

इदं मम महद् दुःखं वर्तते हृदि नित्यदा ।
कृत्वा ज्ञातिक्षयमिमं महान्तं लोभकारितम् ॥ 12.1.14

idaṁ mama mahad duḥkhaṁ vartate hridi nityadā
kritvā jñātiksayamimam mahāntam lobhakāritam
—12.1.14

Simple meaning—Yudhisthira lamented, "O how unhappy I am that because of my greed, so many of my near and dear ones lost their lives."

सौभद्रं द्रौपदेयांश्च घातयित्वा सुतान् प्रियान् ।
जयोऽयमजयाकारो भगवन् प्रतिभाति मे ॥ 12.1.15

saubhadraṁ draupadeyāṁśca ghātayitvā sutān priyān
jayoyamajayākāro bhagavan pratibhāti me
—12.1.15

Simple meaning—"All our sons—born of Draupadi, as well as Abhimanyu, born of Subhadra—have been killed by the Kauravas. I feel, therefore, that defeat, not victory, has come to me."

पूर्वजं भ्रातरं कर्णं पृथाया वचनात् प्रभो ।
तेन मे दूयते तीव्रं हृदयं भ्रातृघातिनः ॥ 12.1.38

pūrvajaṁ bhrātaraṁ karnaṁ prithāyā vacanāt prabho
tena me dūyate tīvraṁ hridayaṁ bhrātrighātinaḥ
—12.1.38

Simple meaning—"I never knew that Karna was my mother's first child—she told me only after Karna had been killed by Arjuna. How unlucky I am that I got my own elder brother killed, due to ignorance."

6.6. Although we have quoted above only a small part of Yudhisthira's lamentation, it is enough to show that, as a result of the war, there was not a single surviving member of their next generation who could succeed Yudhisthira on the throne. Arjuna's grandson, Pariksita, who was born later, gradually grew up to take charge. The tragic chain of events prompted Mahatma Gandhi to draw the following conclusion: "The author of the Mahabharata has not established the necessity of physical warfare; on the contrary he has proved its futility. He has made the victors shed tears of sorrow and repentance, and has left them nothing but a legacy of miseries... In this great work the Gita is the crown.... But if the Gita believed in non-violence, why did the author take a war-like illustration? When the Gita was written, although people believed in non-violence, wars were not only not taboo, but nobody observed the contradiction between them and non-violence."[1]

6.7. In order to console Yudhisthira, the great teachers viz. Vyasa and Lord Krishna began talking with him, and this did have a soothing impact. However, since Yudhisthira still wanted to ask many more questions, Lord Krishna arranged a sort of training for him to be imparted by Bhisma.

6.8. But how did Bhisma acquire the status of a great teacher like Vyasa and Lord Krishna? As we mentioned in para 5.14, Bhisma's conduct in the early part of the Mahabharata was not free from blemish. In Raja-dharma, when Lord Krishna suggested to Bhisma that he may please answer Yudhisthira's questions, Bhisma himself narrated his weaknesses:

दौर्बल्यात् सज्जते वाङ् मे स कथं वक्तुमुत्सहे ।
किं चाहमभिधास्यामि वाक्यं ते तव संनिधौ ॥ 12.52.9

daurbalyāt sajjate vān me sa kathaṁ vaktumutsahe
kiṁ cāhamabhidhāsyāmi vākyaṁ te tava sannidhau
—12.52.9

Simple meaning—Bhisma said to Lord Krishna, "I feel very weak now, and I am aware of my earlier weaknesses too. Furthermore, in your presence, what authority do I have to answer Yudhisthira's questions?"

6.9. But Lord Krishna wanted Bhisma to get rid of all his weaknesses, and to become a great teacher:

आधेयं तु मया भूयो यशस्तव महाद्युते ।
ततो मे विपुला बुद्धिस्त्वयि भीष्म समर्पिता ॥ 12.54.27

ādheyaṁ tu mayā bhūyo yaśastava mahādyute
tato me vipulā buddhistvayi bhīṣma samarpita
—12.54.27

Simple meaning—Lord Krishna said to Bhisma, "I want that you should become a well-known teacher. For this purpose, I am bestowing on you 'vipula buddhi' i.e. broad-mindedness."

It is useful to recall that in para 4.4, "alpa-buddhi" meant "narrow-mindedness" which led to breaking of peace. The opposite of that is "vipula buddhi" i.e. broad-mindedness which can make one a peace-promoter.

यच्च त्वं वक्ष्यसे भीष्म पाण्डवायानुपृच्छते ।
वेदप्रवाद इव ते स्थास्यते वसुधातले ॥ 12.54.29

yacca tvaṁ vaksyase bhīsma pāndavāyanupricchate
vedapravāda iva te sthāsyate vasudhātale
—12.54.29

Simple meaning—After bestowing "vipula buddhi" on Bhisma, Lord Krishna assured him that "Whatever reply you will give to Yudhisthira, in response to his question, that will be recognized as valid as the Vedas."

6.10. In view of the above, it is clear that Yudhisthira received, in Raja-dharma, advice from three great teachers viz. Vyasa, Lord Krishna, and Bhisma. We will derive therefrom, main messages of peace for consideration by Governments.

Main messages given to Yudhisthira in Raja-dharma

6.11. Since messages were given to Yudhisthira in response to his questions, the sequence of these messages needs to be adjusted so as to make them more orderly and effective. When we do so, we find that the first seventy-five per cent of the messages are focused on lokasamgraha (good of all), and that the last twenty-five per cent are focused on world peace. This does not mean that problems of world peace were given a low priority—rather the implication is that only those governments can contribute to world peace which implement lokasamgraha-oriented policies within their territories.

6.12. Message number one. Give up the idea of committing suicide.

Yudhisthira, in a mood of depression and repentance, felt like committing suicide:

सर्वे मामनुजानीत त्यक्ष्यामीदं कलेवरम् ॥ 12.27.27

sarve māmanujānīta tyaksyāmīdaṁ kalevaram
—12.27.27

Simple meaning—Yudhisthira said, "All of you please let me end my life."

However, Vyasa advised Yudhisthira strongly, to give up such a silly idea:

एवमात्मपरित्यागस्तव राजन् न शोभनः ॥ 12.32.23
एवमप्यशुभं कर्म कर्मणस्तत्फलात्मकम् ॥ 12.32.22
विहितानि हि कौन्तेय प्रायश्चित्तानि कर्मणाम् ।
शरीरवांस्तानि कुर्यादशरीरः पराभवेत् ॥ 12.32.24

evamātmaparityāgastava rājan na śobhanaḥ
—12.32.23
evamapyashubhaṁ karma karmaṇastatphalātmakam
—12.32.22
vihitāni hi kaunteya prāyaścittāni karmaṇām
śarīravāṁstāni kuryādaśarīraḥ parābhavet
—12.32.24

Simple meaning—Vyasa said, "O Yudhisthira, the words that you have spoken are unworthy of you—in fact, you should feel ashamed that you thought of committing suicide. You should view your present mood to commit suicide as a part of a chain of events. In your case, one improper action has led to another improper action, and so on. But this chain can be broken if you change your mood now and give up the idea of committing suicide. In that case, you can take new (proper) action to make amends for mistakes made earlier. But if you commit suicide, then you will yourself put an end to chances of taking new (proper) action."

We need not show what further arguments Vyasa gave-instead we give the result viz. that Yudhisthira gave up the idea of committing suicide.

6.13. Message number two. No escapism i.e. do not run away from your social responsibilities.

Yudhisthira expressed a desire to become a monk:

या: काश्चिज्जीवता शक्या: कर्तुमभ्युदयक्रिया: ।
सर्वास्ता: समभित्यज्य निमेषादिव्यवस्थित: ॥ 12.9.26

yāḥ kāscijjīvatā śakyāḥ kartumabhyudaya kriyāḥ
sarvāstaḥ samabhityajya nimeṣādivyavasthitaḥ
—12.9.26

Simple meaning—Yudhisthira declared, "I want to become a monk i.e. withdraw myself from the performance of those acts which benefit the society—even out of those acts which benefit the individual, I shall perform the minimum, for example, open and shut my eyes, and take a little food and drink to stay alive."

The right person to give the right message in such a situation was Lord Krishna who had faced a similar situation in regard to Arjuna in the beginning of the Gita. Krishna now spoke to Yudhisthira:

हतशिष्टाश्च राजान : कृत्स्नं चैव समागतम् ।
चातुर्वर्ण्यं महाराज राष्ट्रं ते कुरुजांगलम् ॥ 12.37.23
सुहृदामस्मदादीनां द्रौपद्याश्च परन्तप ।
कुरु प्रियममित्रघ्न लोकस्य च हितं कुरु ॥ 12.37.25

hataśiṣṭāsca rājānaḥ kritsnaṁ caiva samāgatam
cāturvarnyaṁ mahārāja rāṣṭraṁ te kurujāngalam
—12.37.23

suhridāmasmadādīnāṁ draupadyāśca parantapa
kuru priyamamitraghna lokasya ca hitaṁ kuru
—12.37.25

Simple meaning—Lord Krishna said, "O Yudhisthira, you know that most of the kings died in the war, but some of them did survive - they are looking up to you for the leadership role. All the people of the kingdom that you have won are also looking up to you for help. In this situation, how can you run away from your responsibilities? You should not ignore the advice that you are getting from your wife and your friends. Above all, don't forget that, as a king, you must do lokasaṁgraha (good of all)."

We should mention, as we did in regard to the preceding message, as to what happened next. Raja-dharma tells us that Lord Krishna's advice was accepted by Yudhisthira:

एवमुक्तः स कृष्णेन राजा राजीवलोचनः ।
हितार्थं सर्वलोकस्य समुत्तस्थौ महामनाः ॥ —12.37.26

evamuktaḥ sa krisṇena rājā rājīvalocanaḥ
hitārthaṁ sarvalokasya samuttasthau mahāmanāḥ
—12.37.26

Simple meaning—Vaisampayana says, "Lord Krishna's words had a magic effect. Yudhisthira stood up and declared immediately, 'Here I am, committed and devoted wholeheartedly to lokasamgraha (good of all).'

6.14. Message number three. Give up gambling and let no one scoff at others as Bhima had done to Duryodhana thirteen years ago.

This message is linked to para 5.10—there the two mistakes of the Pandavas (committed thirteen years ago) are pointed out, because of which they too were partly responsible for the war. Thereafter, Yudhisthira was made aware of his mistakes by Lord Krishna (reference para 5.11). The Mahabharata says that, after the war, even without a fresh reminder, Yudhisthira remembered the message given to him by Lord Krishna, and acted accordingly:

न चाप्यवहसन् कंचिन्न कुर्वन् रुचिं द्यूते च ॥ 12.9.17
न बन्धूनवमन्यते स राज्ञो धर्म उच्यते ॥ 12.91.31
आधिर्नास्ति मनुष्याणां व्यसने नाभवन्मतिः ॥ 14.14.22

na cāpyavahasan kancinna kurvan rucim̐ dyūte ca
—12.9.17
na bandhūnavamanyate sa rājño dharma ucyate
—12.91.31
ādhirnāsti manuṣyāṇām̐ vyasane nābhavanmatiḥ
—14.14.22

Simple meaning—Yudhisthira decided that he will not let any one scoff at others nor take any interest in gambling. He knew that, to show disrespect to near and dear ones was contrary to raja-dharma (duties of a king). That is why, in his kingdom, all the citizens developed harmonious relationships, and no one suffered from mental disorder or addiction to gambling, etc.

6.15. Message number four. Protect and nurture all the people living in the state, without any type of discrimination based on faith, sex, urban-rural residence, etc.

The different aspects of this multi-dimensional message are conveyed to Yudhisthira in different contexts of raja-dharma, out of which we present here only five short statements (to avoid giving too much space to any particular message):

एष एव परो धर्मो यद् राजा रक्षति प्रजाः ॥ 12.71.26
न तु भयमुत्पद्यते सैन्येन ह्यभिरक्षणात् ॥ 12.59.122
यस्य स्फीतो जनपद : सम्पन्नो निर्भयः सुखी ॥ 12.94.3
पौरजानपदाश्चैव साम्यरूपेण पालिताः ॥ 12.91.47
सर्वान् देवान् नमस्यन्ति सर्वधर्मांश्च शृण्वते ॥ 12.110.18

eṣa eva paro dharmo yad rājā raksati prajāḥ
—12.71.26

na tu bhayamutpadyate sainyena hyabhirakṣanāt
—12.59.122

yasya sphīto janapadaḥ sampanno nirbhayaḥ sukhī
—12.94.3

paurajānapadāścaiva sāmyarūpeṇa pālitāḥ
—12.91.47

sarvān devān namasyanti sarvadharmāṁśca śriṇvate
—12.110.18

Simple meaning—The most important duty of a king is to protect all the people living within the boundaries of the state. The king can give a real feeling of security and fearlessness to all because he maintains an army for purposes of self-defence. He also ensures prosperity and happiness to all his people—and this will be possible if the size of the state is not too small. He gives a guarantee that there will be no discrimination based on faith, sex, urban-rural residence, etc.

6.16. Message number five. To all those who are orphans, oppressed or too weak to take care of themselves, the king should make arrangements to provide the necessary support and whenever possible, to enable them to stand on their own feet, after receiving training as well as resources.

This message too, like the preceding one, is conveyed to Yudhisthira in different contexts of raja-dharma, out of which we present here only three statements :

अभृतानां भवेद् भर्ता भृतानामन्ववेक्षकः ॥ 12.57.19

आर्तहस्तप्रदो नित्यमाप्तामात्यो नये रतः ॥ 12.118.19

संविभज्य यदा भुंक्ते नृपतिर्दुर्बलान् नरान्।
तदा भवन्ति बलिनः स राज्ञो घर्म उच्यते ॥ 12.91.33

abhritānāṁ bhaved bhartā bhritānāmanvavekṣakaḥ
—12.57.19

ārtahastaprado nityamāptāmātyo naye rataḥ
—12.118.19

saṁvibhajya yadā bhunkte nripatirdurbalān narān
tadā bhavanti balinaḥ sa rājño dharma ucyate
—12.91.33

Simple meaning—To orphans and others who have no one to look after them, welfare organizations funded by the king should provide support and the work of these organizations should also be properly supervised to ensure that real help reaches the needy. Those who are in distress or oppressed, should be given assurance of help, and only those ministers who are sympathetic to their needs, should be made responsible for such help. The policy of helping the weak should depend, not on giving doles or charity, but rather on sharing the resources and on raising the level of their skills, so that they can stand on their own feet, after receiving the training and the resources.

6.17. Message number six. Give honor to old people and make special arrangements to satisfy their health and psychological needs. Yudhisthira accepted this message spontaneously and declared his respect for Dhritarastra.

कृपणानाथवृद्धानां दुर्बलातुरयोषिताम् ।
संविभक्तास्तु सर्वेषामश्रु च परिमार्जयन् ॥ —12.77.18
वृद्धसेवी महोत्साहः सम्मानदो यथायोग्यम् ॥ —12.118.29
धृतराष्ट्रो महाराज : पिता मे दैवतं परम् ।
अस्य शुश्रूषणं कार्यं मया नित्यमतंद्रिणा ॥ —12.41.4

kripaṇānāthavriddhānāṁ durbalāturayoṣitām
saṁvibhaktāstu sarveṣāmaśru ca parimārjayan
—12.77.18
vriddhasevī mahotsāhaḥ sammānado yathāyogyam
—12.118.29
dhritarāṣṭro mahārājaḥ pitā me daivataṁ param
asya śuśrūṣaṇaṁ kāryaṁ mayā nityamatandriṇā
—12.41.4

Simple meaning—Share the prosperity of the state with all those who reside there, including the old and the weak (paying special attention to women) and satisfy their health and psychological needs. For this purpose, serve the old people enthusiastically, and respectfully. Yudhisthira's spontaneous acceptance of this message is clear from his declaration, "The great king

Dhritarastra is like my father and all the time I consider it my duty to serve him respectfully."

6.18. Message number seven. Whatever policy decisions you want to take, as a follow-up of the exemplary rulers of the past, keep in mind the importance of making the necessary adjustments or changes in the traditional concepts, corresponding to changes in time, place and circumstances.

This is the famous 'desh-kala-patra' message of the Gita (reference para 4.32) and the Mahabharata has re-affirmed it, several times in raja-dharma. We present here only two verses therefrom:

धृतिर्दाक्ष्यं संयमो बुद्धिरात्मा
धैर्यं शौर्यं देशकालाप्रमादः ॥ 12.120.37
देशकालविधानज्ञान् नृपकार्यहितैषिणः ।
नित्यमर्थेषु सर्वेषु राजा कुर्वीत मंत्रिणः ॥ 12.83.8

dhritirdākṣyaṁ saṁyamo buddhirātmā
dhairyaṁ śauryaṁ deśakālāpramādaḥ —12.120.37
deśakālavidhānajñān nripakāryahitaiṣiṇaḥ
nityamartheṣu sarveṣu rājā kurvīta mantriṇah
—12.83.8

Simple meaning—Among the desired qualifications of a king, his willingness to make policies in the light of the 'desh-kala-patra' message has an important place. (The other qualities mentioned here include: patience, fearlessness, self-discipline, and efficiency).

Among the desired qualifications of ministers also, their ability to implement the 'desh-kala-patra' policy has an important place. (The other qualities mentioned here include: commitment to complete the tasks assigned by the king, and desire to do good to all the people).

This message has been assigned number seven, in the sequence planned by us, because an important application of this can be in the field of education which comes next in the sequence.

6.19. Message number eight. Give the right education to all and let this be the primary way to cultivate right values in the society (including the strengthening of fellow-feeling among all the people).

Raja-dharma advises Yudhisthira to follow the examples of great kings of the past, after making the necessary adjustments or changes in what they did, corresponding to changes in time, place and circumstances. In the field of education, the finest example is that of King Asvapati, who arranged for giving the right education to all, as is clear from his statement in Chandogya Upanisad (Please see para 5.25):

न मे स्तेनो जनपदे न कदर्यो न मद्यपः ।
नानाहिताग्निर्नाविद्वान्न स्वैरी स्वैरिणी कुतः ॥ छां० उप० 5.11.5

na me steno janapade na kadaryo na madyapaḥ
nānāhitāgnirnāvidvānna svairī svairiṇī kutaḥ
—ch.up. 5.11.5

Simple meaning—This mantra (hymn) describes the happy state of affairs achieved by Asvapati's administration, the main points relevant to message number eight being:

(i) there was no thief, no miser, no drunkard
(ii) there was no uneducated
(iii) there was no instance of adulterous affair between men and women.

The achievement of Yudhisthira's administration in the field of education is indicated in the Asvamedha Parva of the Mahabharata:

सर्वे नराश्च नार्यश्च सततं प्रियवादिनः ।
अजिह्ममनसः शुक्ला बभूवु विद्यासम्पन्नाः ॥ —14.14.28

sarve narāśca nāryaśca satatam priyavādinaḥ
ajihmamanasaḥ śuklā babhūvu vidyāsampannāḥ
—14.14.28

Simple meaning—As a result of having received the right education, all the men and women in Yudhisthira's kingdom developed purity of heart, and they wanted to do good to others, by thought, word and deed.

6.20. Message number nine. Increase food production in the country and try to make all the people healthy and prosperous.

This message is based on Raja-dharma's description of the achievements of another exemplary ruler of the past, viz. Prithu:

अकृष्टपच्या पृथिवी पुटके पुटके मधु ।
अरोगा: सर्वसिद्धार्था मनुष्या अकुतोभया: ॥ 12.29.140

akriṣṭapacyā prithivī puṭake puṭake madhu
arogāḥ sarvasiddhārthā manuṣyā akutobhayāḥ
—12.29.140

Simple meaning—During Prithu's rule, the earth yielded crops, as if without being tilled. The production of honey was plentiful too. The people enjoyed excellent health and had all their wishes fulfilled—so they had no fear of any kind.

The Asvamedha Parva says that the achievements of Yudhisthira's administration were similar:

मही सस्यप्रबहुला सर्वरत्नगुणोदया ॥ 14.14.42
निरामयं जगदभूत् क्षुत्पिपासे न किंचन ॥ 14.14.21

mahī sasyaprabahulā sarvaratnaguṇodayā
—14.14.42
nirāmayaṁ jagadabhūt kṣutpipāse na kincana
—14.14.21

Simple meaning—During Yudhisthira's rule, the earth yielded bountiful crops as well as precious stones. Good food and pure water helped people stay healthy.

6.21. Message number ten. Take effective measures to protect the environment, for example, by planting and protecting trees.

Raja-dharma contains a specific advice to Yudhisthira, to protect trees (Please see para 5.26):

वनस्पतीन् भक्ष्यफलान्
न च्छिन्द्युर्विषये तव ॥ —12.89.1

vanaspatīn bhaksyaphalān
na cchindyurviṣaye tava —12.89.1

Simple meaning—As a king you should ensure that plants and trees which yield edible fruits should not be cut down in your kingdom.

Asvamedha Parva says that Yudhisthira's administration did follow the above advice:

स्थावरा बहुपुष्पाढ्या : फलच्छायावहास्तथा ।
सुस्पर्शा विषहीनाश्च सुपत्रत्वंक्प्ररोहिण: ॥ —14.14.37

sthāvarā bahupuṣpādhyāḥ phalacchāyāvahāstathā
susparśā viṣahīnāśca supatratvakprarohiṇaḥ
—14.14.37

Simple meaning—Yudhisthira's kingdom abounded in plants and trees that had beautiful flowers, yielded fruits, and provided shade to pedestrians. These were poison-free, and people enjoyed picnicking in that healthy environment.

6.22. Message number eleven. Raise the status of women in the society, by empowering them through higher education, as Asvapati did for his daughter Savitri.

Asvapati's own example, in the field of education, was given in message number eight (para 6.19). Now, Asvapati's daughter Savitri is presented as an exemplary woman. Her story is narrated in the Mahabharata in great detail, but we give below a summarized version thereof:

Savitri grew up as a highly educated woman, who was unsurpassed in beauty, wisdom and virtue. Awed by her radiance, no one came forward to seek her hand. So her father asked her to go to different places to find a suitable match for herself.

Savitri travelled to various places and finally succeeded in her mission. When she returned to her father to make the announcement, the sage Narada happened to be there. Savitri said, in front of all, 'I have identified Satyavan as my husband-to-be. His father Dyumatsena used to be a king, but suddenly he became blind, so a neighbouring ruler deprived Dyumatsena of his kingdom. He now lives in the woods, with his wife and son (i.e. Satyavan).'

Narada (who could read the future also) said that Satyavan has all the qualities to match Savitri's, but his life's span will come to an end after one year.

However, Savitri's resolve was not shaken, and her marriage with Satyavan was performed at a simple ceremony in the woods.

On the fateful day, one year later (as predicted by Narada), Yama, the god of death, arrived in the woods to take Satyavan's life. Savitri was able to see Yama because of the strength of her character. Then a long conversation between Yama and Savitri took place. Words spoken by Savitri about the importance of friendliness and of doing good to all, pleased Yama so much that he asked Savitri to specify five boons which he will grant. Savitri listed the boons that she wanted, in the following order:

(a) restoration of her father-in-law's eye-sight
(b) restoration of her father-in-law's sovereignty over his former kingdom.
(c) that her parents may have sons
(d) prolongation of Satyavan's life
(e) granting moral strength to her parents as well as to her husband so that the whole family may promote social harmony.

Yama granted all the boons. In this way, Savitri was able to alter Narada's prediction about her husband's death, and she became instrumental in promoting not only the welfare of the entire family, but also social harmony.

Now, a sample of the words that Savitri had spoken to Yama:

सौहृदात् सर्वभूतानां विश्वासो नाम जायते ॥ 3.297.43
संत : परार्थं कुर्वाणा नावेक्षन्ति परस्परम् ॥ 3.297.49
संतस्त्वेवाप्यमित्रेषु दयां प्राप्तेषु कुर्वते ॥ 3.297.36
संतो भूमिं तपसा धारयन्ति ॥ 3.297.48

sauhridāt sarvabhūtānāṁ viśvāso nāma jāyate
—3.297.43

santaḥ parārthaṁ kurvāṇā nāvekṣanti parasparam
—3.297.49

santastvevāpyamitreṣu dayāṁ prāpteṣu kurvate
—3.297.36

santo bhūmiṁ tapasā dhārayanti —3.297.48

Simple meaning—To be friendly towards all—this is the best way to establish mutual trust and to keep the society united.

Peace-promoters do good to others without expecting any benefit for themselves in return. They show compassion, even to their foes when they (i.e. the foes) are in a mood to make peace.

Peace in the world is attainable if more and more people become compassionate.

6.23. Message number twelve. While choosing ministers and advisers, look for their commitment to peace, and keep in mind the example of Vidura, who advised Dhritarastra when the latter was a king.

Raja-dharma contains detailed advice about choosing the right persons, to occupy positions of ministers and advisers. For our present purpose, the most important piece of advice is contained in the following verse:

मंत्रिणो यस्य सन्तश्च स्वनागतविधातारः ॥ —12.115.16

mantriṇo yasya santaśca svanāgatavidhātāraḥ
—12.115.16

Simple meaning—Ministers should be peace-loving to start with, and they should be further trained to promote peace in the context of new problems that cannot be predicted.

As a visible example of the right adviser, Vidura's name was highlighted—Vidura had advised Dhritarastra when the latter was a king, and Vidura was still alive (although retired). (Please see para 5.20).

By birth, Vidura was a sudra (i.e. of low social status), but he was so righteous that the Mahabharata depicted him as an incarnation of Dharma. The birth of Dharma in a sudra family is explained by means of the following story. Risi Mandavya had his ashrama (hermitage) near a city. Some robbers, when pursued by king's men, hid themselves in that ashrama, without the knowledge of the Risi who was immersed in deep meditation. The king's men arrested the robbers and the Risi too, and the king punished all of them, without ascertaining whether the Risi had any connection with the robbery. Mandavya asked Dharma, the divine dispenser of justice, why he (i.e. the Risi) had to suffer at the hands of the king. Dharma told Mandavya that he (i.e. the latter) had tortured birds and bees in his childhood. The Risi then pronounced a curse on Dharma, 'You gave me punishment far in excess of what I should have received for my childhood delinquency. Be born, therefore, as a sudra in the world.'

Vidura's advice to Dhritarastra is spread over eight chapters, but we present below only two verses therefrom:

सुलभाः पुरुषा राजन् सततं प्रियवादिनः ।
अप्रियस्य तु पथ्यस्य वक्ता श्रोता च दुर्लभः ॥ —5.37.15
न तत् परस्य संदध्यात् प्रतिकूलं यदात्मनः ।
संग्रहेणैष धर्मं स्यात् कामादन्यः प्रवर्तते ॥ —5.39.71

sulabhāḥ puruṣā rājan satataṁ priyavādinaḥ
apriyasya tu pathyasya vaktā śrotā ca durlabhaḥ
—5.37.15

na tat parasya sandadhyāt pratikūlaṁ yadātmanaḥ
sangraheṇaiṣa dharmam syāt kāmādanyaḥ pravartate
—5.39.71

Simple meaning—O King, there are plenty of people who will say to you what pleases you. However, it is difficult to find a person who will say what, though unpleasant, will do good to you and similarly, a listener to such words is also difficult to find.

That behaviour, which is disagreeable to one's own self, should never be applied to others. This is the essence of dharma (righteousness). Whatever is contrary to this, is based on selfishness (and is therefore unrighteous).

6.24. Message number thirteen. Since you cannot take for granted that anti-social elements will not commit violence against the people and property of your country, you should maintain your self-defence capability, which depends jointly on your military strength, and a feeling of unity among the people brought about by your lokasamgraha-policies.

Parts of this message are contained in the messages already given, but the importance of a purposeful coordination of the various messages is highlighted here.

एष एव परो धर्मो यद् राजा रक्षति प्रजाः । —12.71.26
न तु भयमुत्पद्यते सैन्येन ह्यभिरक्षणात् ॥ —12.59.122
राज्ञो रहस्यं बोद्धव्यं जयार्थं लोकसंग्रहः ॥ —12.58.19
यस्य स्फीतो जनपदः सम्पन्नो निर्भयः सुखी ।
संतुष्टपुष्टसचिवो दृढमूलः स पार्थिवः ॥ —12.94.3

eṣa eva paro dharmo yad rājā rakṣati prajāḥ
—12.71.26
na tu bhayamutpadyate sainyena hyabhirakṣanāt
—12.59.122
rājño rahasyaṁ boddhavyaṁ jayārthaṁ lokasaṁgrahaḥ
—12.58.19
yasya sphīto janapadaḥ sampanno nirbhayaḥ sukhī
santuṣṭapūṣṭasacivo driḍhamūlaḥ sa pārthivaḥ
—12.94.3

Simple meaning—The most important duty of a king is to protect all the people within the boundaries of the state. The king can give a real feeling of security and fearlessness to all because of two things: (a) he maintains an army for purposes of self-defence, (b) he follows lokasamgraha-policies to bring about all-round development of the country. In fact, the intrinsic strength of the country depends on the prosperity, happiness and unity of all the people and the commitment, honesty and efficiency of the administration.

6.25. Message number fourteen. Whatever disputes you might have with the governments of other countries, take a firm policy decision that you will settle them peacefully, because wars cannot provide a satisfactory solution to any dispute.

The Mahabharata contains this explicit message, and also a statement that Yudhisthira's administration acted in accordance with this message.

अयुद्धेनैव विजयं वर्धयेद् वसुधाधिपः ।
जघन्यमाहुर्विजयं युद्धेन च नराधिप ॥ —12.94.1
असाधून् साधुना जयेत् ॥ —12.95.16
विजिते पाण्डवै राजन् प्रशान्ते च विशाम्पते ।
राष्ट्रे बभूवतुर्हृष्टौ वासुदेवधनंजयौ ॥ —14.15.2

ayuddhenaiva vijayaṁ vardhayed vasudhādhipaḥ
jaghanyamāhurvijayaṁ yuddhena ca narādhipa
—12.94.1
asādhūn sādhunā jayet —12.95.16
vijite pāndavai rājan praśānte ca viśāmpate
rāṣṭre babhūvaturhriṣṭau vāsudevadhananjayau
—14.15.2

Simple meaning—Raja-dharma gives this message to Yudhisthira: "O King, in order to achieve success in your policy towards other governments, use only peaceful means, because solutions of disputes through wars are never satisfactory.

Victory over anti-social elements can, and should be, achieved by peaceful methods.

Subsequently, Asvamedha Parva says, "After Yudhisthira won the Mahabharata war, his administration followed a policy of peace-and Lord Krishna as well as Arjuna felt happy with the success of that policy."

6.26. Message number fifteen. Follow the example of Indra who insisted that everyone will follow only the commander-in-chief Kartikeya—similarly, you should not allow any private army in your kingdom.

Glorification of Kartikeya by the Mahabharata has been referred to in para 5.30. The present message is based on Indra's declaration that only the commander-in-chief (Kartikeya) will be followed (i.e there will be no private army).

शतक्रतुश्चाभिषिच्य स्कन्दं सेनापतिं तदा ॥ —3.229.44
अनुयातः सुरैः सर्वैः कार्तिकेयपुरोगमैः ॥ —3.231.29
यथामुखान् संनिपात्य वक्तव्याः संशपामहे ।
विजयार्थं हि संग्रामे न त्यक्ष्यामः परस्परम् ॥ —12.100.32

śatakratuścābhiṣicya skandaṁ senāpatiṁ tadā
—3.229.44
anuyātaḥ suraiḥ sarvaiḥ kārtikeyapurogamaiḥ
—3.231.29
yathāmukhān sannipātya vaktavyāḥ saṁśapāmahe
vijayārthaṁ hi sangrāme na tyakṣyāmaḥ parasparam
—12.100.32

Simple meaning—On behalf of all the gods, Indra announced that Kartikeya (also known as Skanda or Kumar) is our commander-in-chief and that everyone will follow him wholeheartly.

Similarly, the king, after appointing the commander-in-chief must obtain a firm assurance from all the military personnel that they will not betray the commander-in-chief (by forming a separate, private army).

6.27. Message number sixteen. You should ensure that no donation or help or support of any kind is given to anti-social elements.

Raja-dharma has given this message, several times, in different contexts. We give below two verses, one supporting this message from the dharma-angle, and the second from the patra-angle (i.e. who deserves to be supported and who does not deserve)—(we have composed the second verse by summarizing and bringing together, several of the Mahabharata-verses):

न वै देयमनुक्रोशाद् दीनायाप्यपकारिणे ।
आप्ताचरित इत्येव धर्म इत्येव वा पुनः ॥ 12.36.44
दानं साहाय्यप्रदानं देयं केवलं पात्रेभ्यः ।
त्यक्तनीतये तद्रूपं संज्ञितमसहकारम् ॥

na vai deyamanukrośād dīnāyāpyapakāriṇe
āptācarita ityeva dharma ityeva vā punaḥ
—12.36.44
dānaṁ sāhāyyapradānaṁ deyaṁ kevalaṁ pātrebhyaḥ
tyaktanītaye tadrūpaṁ sanjñitamasahakāram

***Simple meaning*—**Those who do harm to others should not be given any money or help, even if they say that they are poor. Help given to anti-social elements is not considered to be compassion, by dharma-scholars.

Four messages have been summarized and brought together, in the second verse: (a) The act of giving includes not only money but also any help or cooperation, (b) Give only to one who deserves—and never to one who is anti-social, (c) One who has gone astray from the path of peace does not deserve anything and (d) Therefore don't give any co-operation to anti-social elements., *e.g.* don't allow them to use the country's territory for peace-breaking activities.

Potential applications of these messages in the context of the twenty-first century

6.28. Out of all the messages that Yudhisthira received, the one given in para 6.25 has a special, potential application in the twenty-first century. In order to specify this, we first recall and rephrase the message: "Whatever disputes a government might have with the governments of other countries, it should take a firm policy decision to settle them peacefully, because wars cannot provide a satisfactory solution to any dispute."

The most useful application of this message in the twenty-first century would be to inspire the governments to strengthen their commitment to world peace by enhancing what we can call their "World Peace Promotion Preparedness." A systematic way of doing this could be to prepare a WPPP (World Peace Promotion Preparedness) Index with the help of a self-administered check-list.

Items included in the check-list are essentially the messages given in this chapter, to be supplemented by some of the messages of the next two chapters. The total number of messages may preferably be at least twenty-five, and the WPPP Index for any government would be the percentage of those messages to which that government is prepared to give a 'yes' reply. Of course, the most appropriate organization to give a final shape to the concept of WPPP Index is the United Nations. Once the relevant procedure is set in motion, the UN could then put invisible pressure on those governments which have a relatively lower WPPP Index, to find out ways of raising that index in the years to come. Delicate issues (like replacing peacefully, a dictatorship by a democratic set-up, and a theocracy by a secular set-up) which cannot by themselves be easily raised with the concerned governments, could form a part of WPPP Index.

6.29. Another message with a great, potential application relates to education (reference para 6.19). Again we recall and rephrase the message first, before specifying its application: "Strong governmental support should be given to programs which seek to give the right education to all the children (i.e. boys as well as girls), and which seek to use education to cultivate right values in the society including the strengthening of fellow-feeling among the people following different faiths."

As an application of this message, the government should officially declare that one of the aims of education will be to prepare the minds of students so that they become fit to be peace-loving citizens of the world. In pursuance of this aim, all the students will be given broad-based education and they will also be taught how to use their knowledge for the benefit of mankind. Such teaching should also emphasize and ensure that no student will use his or her knowledge to destroy world peace. If necessary, the governments may seek technical assistance from UNESCO so that they can plan for all-round educational development, and also implement such plans as quickly and smoothly as possible.

6.30. For one more application, the message given in para 5.36 presents a challenging but very important task, in respect of those governments which are dictatorial. Again we recall the message of para 5.36:

"United Nations can draw a lesson from the Mahabharata and take necessary action to replace dictatorial governments by democracies, in the interest of world peace. Of course, the cooperation of the concerned governments will be needed, for a peaceful change, from dictatorship to democracy."

The applicational aspect of this message is already covered under the WPPP Index explained in para 6.28.

6.31. Another challenging application, similar to the one mentioned in the preceding para, can be inferred from paras 3.15 and 5.23. The task involved in the present case is in respect of those governments which are theocratic, and which need to be replaced by a secular set-up, by peaceful means. Again we recall and rephrase the message of paras 3.15 and 5.23:

"The biggest contribution to world peace can be made by those countries that are secular democracies. Therefore, United Nations would be very much interested in replacing a theocratic set-up (wherever it exists) by a secular set-up. Of course, the cooperation of the concerned government will be needed for a peaceful change."

Like the message of the preceding para, the applicational aspect of this message too is already covered under the WPPP Index explained in para 6.28.

CHAPTER 7

Mahabharata's Messages of Peace for Consideration by Religious Leaders

7.1. The preceding chapter presented the Mahabharata's messages of peace for consideration by governments. Those messages were based on the raja-dharma section of Shanti-Parva. In this chapter, we will give the Mahabharata's messages of peace for consideration by religious leaders. The main source of these messages is the moksa-dharma section of Shanti-Parva.

7.2. Following the pattern of the preceding chapter, this chapter too will consist of three main sections:

(a) Re-affirmation, by moksa-dharma, of the sixteen main messages given to Yudhisthira in raja-dharma (i.e. the messages presented in chapter six).

(b) Additional messages of peace given to Yudhisthira in moksa-dharma.

(c) Potential applications of these messages in the context of the twenty-first century.

Re-affirmation of the messages given in chapter six

7.3. Message number one. Give up the idea of committing suicide.

Raja-dharma's verses on this topic were presented in para 6.12. Moksa-dharma has devoted one full chapter to this topic. This chapter contains a long dialogue between Indra and Kasyapa, but we give here a short summary thereof. Kasyapa was the son of a sage, but on one occasion, he was insulted and thrown out of a vehicle, by a wealthy but arrogant person. Kasyapa felt so humiliated that he thought of committing suicide:

आर्तः स पतितः क्रुद्धस्त्यक्त्वाऽत्मानमथाब्रवीत् ।
मरिष्याम्यधनस्येह जीवितार्थो न विद्यते ॥ 12.180.6

ārtaḥ sa patitaḥ kruddhastyaktvātmānamathābravīt
mariṣyāmyadhanasyeha jīvitārtho na vidyate
—12.180.6

Simple meaning—Having been thrown out of the vehicle, by a wealthy and arrogant person, Kasyapa felt oppressed and dejected. He said, "For a poor man like me, life in this world is not worth living, so I better put an end to my life."

In order to save the life of Kasyapa, Indra, the chief of gods, assumed the form of a jackal and spoke to him:

अकार्यमिति चैवेमं नात्मानं संत्यजाम्यहम् ॥ —12.180.21
न पुल्कसो न चाण्डाल आत्मानं त्यक्तुमिच्छति ॥ —12.180.38
सुसम्पूर्णः स्वया योन्या लब्धलाभोऽसि काश्यप ॥ —12.180.39
न केनचित् प्रवादेन सत्येनैवापहारिणा ।
धर्मायोत्तिष्ठ विप्रर्षे नात्मानं त्यक्तुमर्हसि ॥ 12.18.41

akāryamiti caivemaṁ nātmānaṁ santyajāmyaham
—12.180.21

na pulkaso na cāṇḍāla ātmānaṁ tyaktumicchati
—12.180.38

susampūrṇaḥ svayā yonyā labdhalabhosi kāsyapa
—12.180.39

na kenacit pravādena satyenaivāpahāriṇā
dharmāyottiṣṭha viprarṣe nātmānam tyaktumarhasi
—12.180.41

Simple meaning—Indra (in the form of a jackal) said, "O Kasyapa, look at me—a jackal whose position is much worse than yours. I never think of committing suicide because I consider it a sin. Amongst human beings, low caste labourers, whose position is worse than yours, do not want to commit suicide. Think coolly and then you will realize that you have received plenty of benefits, more than many in the society. Whatever might be the humiliation that you have suffered, never think of putting an end to your life. Get up and move forward, performing your dharma (duty), rather than lie depressed."

To complete this story, it should be added that Kasyapa was amazed as to how a jackal could be so wise. Then Indra revealed himself. Kasyapa gave up the idea of committing suicide, and got up to carry on his normal duty in life:

ततः सम्पूजयामास काश्यपो हरिवाहनम् ।
अनुज्ञातस्तु तेनाथ प्रविवेश स्वमालयम् ॥ —12.180.54

tataḥ sampūjayāmāsa kāsyapo harivāhanam
anujnātastū tenātha pravivesśa svamālayam
—12.180.54

Simple meaning—Kasyapa expressed his gratefulness to Indra for having saved his life, and then went home, determined to follow Indra's advice.

7.4. Message number two. No escapism i.e. don't run away from your social responsibilities.

Raja-dharma's verses on this topic were presented in para 6.13. Moksa-dharma contains so many verses giving the same message, out of which we give below those which would be particularly appropriate to the story of Kasyapa narrated above (although they belong to two different chapters):

तस्मादेतैरधिक्षिप्तः सहेन्नित्यमसंज्वरः ।
गृहधर्मपरो विद्वान् धर्मशीलो जितक्लमः ॥ —12.243.21

tasmādetairadhikṣiptaḥ sahennityamasanjvarah
grihadharmaparo vidvān dharmasīlo jitaklamaḥ
—12.243.21

Simple meaning—Even if you are insulted by someone, don't feel dejected. Use your knowledge to give you moral strength, and continue looking after your household responsibilities cheerfully.

श्रियाविहीनैरलसैः पण्डितैः सम्प्रवर्तितम् ।
वेदवादापरिज्ञानं सत्याभासमिवानृतम् ॥ —12.269.17

śriyāvihīnairalasaiḥ panditaiḥ sampravartitam
vedavādāparijnānaṁ satyābhāsamivānritam
—12.269.17

Simple meaning—Those pandits (scholars) who advocate monkhood are themselves lazy and of no real use to society—they have no real knowledge of the Vedas and they give wrong advice (although they pretend to give the true message of the Vedas).

यथा मातरमाश्रित्य सर्वे जीवन्ति जन्तवः ।
एवं गार्हस्थ्यमाश्रित्य वर्तन्त इतराश्रमाः ॥ —12.269.6

yathā mātaramāsritya sarve jīvanti jantavaḥ
evaṁ gārhasthyamāsritya vartanta itarāsramāḥ
—12.269.6

Simple meaning—Just as all the living beings primarily depend on their mothers for maintaining themselves, similarly the householders provide the basic support to the other three ashramas (categories) viz. brahmacarya, vanaprastha and sannyasa. In other words, monks too need the support of householders.

गृहस्थ एव यजते गृहस्थस्तप्यते तपः ।
गार्हस्थ्यमस्य धर्मस्य मूलं यत्किंचिदेजते ॥ —12.269.7

grihastha eva yajate grihasthastapyate tapaḥ
gārhasthyamasya dharmasya mūlaṁ yatkincidejate
—12.269.7

Simple meaning—All socially useful activities (which are often depicted as a trio "yajna-danam-tapas") are performed with the help of householders, although the other three categories might appear to be performing them.

7.5. Message number three. Give up gambling and let no one scoff at others as Bhima had done to Duryodhana thirteen years ago.

Raja-dharma's verses on this topic were presented in para 6.14. Moksa-dharma has not only conveyed the same message but has also advised that, rather than lamenting over the mistakes committed in the past, one should make a determined effort to avoid those mistakes in the future:

नाक्षैर्दीव्येन्नाददीतान्यवित्तं
न वायोनीयस्य श्रृतं प्रगृह्णात् ॥ —12.269.24
नाक्रोशमृच्छेन्न वृथा वदेच्च
न पैशुनं परिहासं च कुर्यात् ॥ —12.269.25
तथाप्युपायं सम्पश्येद् दुःखस्य परिमोक्षणम् ।
अशोचन् नारभेच्चैव मुक्तश्चाव्यसनी भवेत् ॥ —12.330.25

nāksairdīvyennādadītānyavittaṁ
na vāyonīyasya śritaṁ pragrihṇāt —12.269.24
nākrosamricchenna vrithā vadecca
na paiśunaṁ parihāsaṁ ca kuryāt —12.269.25
tathāpyupāyaṁ sampasyed duḥkhasya parimoksaṇam
asocan nārabheccaiva muktascāvyasanī bhavet
—12.330.25

Simple meaning—In order to lead a life based on dharma, one should not take interest in gambling, should not try to grab what belongs to others, and should not accept food offered by anti-social people.

Furthermore, one should not speak ill of others, should not utter purposeless words, and should not scoff at others.

Rather than keep on lamenting over the mistakes committed in the past, one should concentrate on what to do now—and make a determined effort to avoid committing the old mistakes in the future.

7.6. Message number four. The king should protect and nurture all the people living in the state, without any type of discrimination based on faith, sex, urban-rural residence, etc.

Raja-dharma's verses on this topic were presented in para 6.15. Moksa-dharma has given the same message by depicting

Janaka as the ideal king. In fact, the exemplary role of Janaka has been referred to in several Parva's of the Mahabharata, and we too have included here a verse from Asvamedha Parva, to supplement Moksa-dharma's narration (Please see para 4.35):

जनकेन प्रतिष्ठिता वसन्ति शतमाचार्या : ।
दर्शयन्ति पृथग्धर्मान् नानास्थाननिवासिन: ॥ —12.218.4
बहुद्वारस्य धर्मस्य कथयन्त्युदारभावम् ॥ —12.174.2
प्रजा: सृष्टा मनसा प्रज्ञया च ।
न स्त्री न च पुमान् भेदरहिता: ॥ —12.201.15
देवेभ्यश्च पितृभ्यश्च भूतेभ्योऽतिथिभि: सह ।
इत्यर्थं सर्व एवेति समारम्भा भवन्ति वै ॥ —14.32.24

janakena pratiṣṭhitā vasanti satamācāryāḥ
darsayanti prithagdharmān nānāsthānanivāsinah
—12.218.4
bahudvārasya dharmasya kathayantyudārabhāvam
—12.174.2
prajāh sriṣṭā manasā prajnayā ca
na strī na ca pumān bhedarahitāḥ —12.201.15
devebhyasca pitribhyasca bhūtebhyotithibhiḥ saha
ityarthaṁ sarva eveti samārambhā bhavanti vai
—14.32.24

Simple meaning—In Janaka's court, there were one hundred spiritual leaders, towards all of whom the king had equal respect—they came from different places, cities and villages, and they explained different aspects of dharma. Janaka was broad-minded and he did not put any restriction on the people who were free to choose their own faith. Janaka believed, similarly, in giving equal opportunities to men and women, who possessed God-given capabilities to enable them to serve the society in their own ways. About his own role, he declared, "All activities of mine are for the benefit of the gods, the ancestors, all created beings (human and others), and my guests, but not for my own selfish benefit."

7.7. Message number five. To all those who are orphans,

oppressed or too weak to take care of themselves, the king should make arrangements to provide the necessary support—and whenever possible, to enable them to stand on their own feet, after receiving training as well as resources.

Raja-dharma's verses on this topic were presented in para 6.16. Moksa-dharma gives the same message to the kings:

त्रस्तं विषण्णमुद्विग्नं भयार्तं व्याधितं कृशम् ।
हृतस्वं व्यसनार्तं च नित्यमाश्वासयन्ति ते ॥ —12.228.41
आश्रित्य संविभागं च प्रीतिपुरोगेन तथा ।
राजधर्मं पालयित्वा बलं सामर्थ्यमददुः ॥ —12.297.35

trastaṁ viṣannamudvignaṁ bhayārtaṁ vyādhitaṁ kriśam
hritasvaṁ vyasanārtaṁ ca nityamāśvāsayanti te
—12.228.41

āśritya saṁvibhāgaṁ ca prītipurogena tathā
rājadharmaṁ pālayitvā balaṁ sāmarthyamadaduh
—12.297.35

Simple meaning—The king should provide support and sympathy to all those who are oppressed, dejected, unhappy, frightened, sick, weak, orphans or victims of bad habits. The best support is to give them a share of the kingdom's prosperity and resources, as well as training imparted with love, to enable them to stand on their own feet, whenever possible.

7.8. Message number six.Give honor to old people and make special arrangements to satisfy their health and psychological needs.

Raja-dharma's verses on this topic were presented in para 6.17. Not only is Moksa-dharma's message the same, but also the words used to convey it are practically the same:

प्रयत्नसाध्यो हि स राजपुत्रः
वृद्धानुपास्य श्रुतिधर्मयुक्तः ॥ —12.297.29
कृपणानाथवृद्धानां दुर्बलातुरयोषिताम् ।
दयां च संविभागं च नित्यमेवान्वमोदताम् ॥ —12.228.40

prayatnasādhyo hi sa rājaputraḥ
vriddhānupāsya srutidharmayuktaḥ —12.297.29
kripaṇānāthavriddhānāṁ durbalāturayoṣitām
dayāṁ ca samvibhāgaṁ ca nityamevānvamodatām
—12.228.40

Simple meaning—Even members of the royal family should make special effort to show respect to old people, in accordance with Vedic dharma. The prosperity of the state should be shared with all those who reside there, including the old and the weak (paying special attention to women)—and their health and psychological needs should be satisfied.

7.9. Message number seven. Whatever policy decisions you want to take, as a follow-up of the exemplary people of the past, keep in mind the importance of making the necessary adjustments or changes in the traditional concepts, corresponding to changes in time, place and circumstances.

Raja-dharma's verses on this topic were presented in para 6.18. Moksa-dharma contains an elaboration of the same message together with a warning that blind adherence to old practices could mean a continuation of out-dated, cruel practices, even if they are no longer relevant:

अन्ये कृतयुगे धर्मास्त्रेतायां द्वापरे परे ।
अन्ये कलियुगे धर्मा यथाकालं प्रतिष्ठिता: ॥ —12.260.8
स एव धर्म : सोऽधर्मस्तं तं प्रतिनरं भवेत् ।
पात्रकर्मविशेषेण देशकालाववेक्ष्य च ॥ —12.309.16
ईदृशानशिवान् घोरानाचारानिह जाजले ।
केवलाचरित्वात् तु निपुणो नावबुद्ध्यसे ॥ —12.262.52

anye kritayuge dharmāstretāyāṁ dvāpare pare
anye kaliyuge dharma yathākālaṁ pratiṣṭhitā
—12.260.8
sa eva dharmaḥ sodharmastaṁ taṁ prati naraṁ bhavet
pātrakarmaviśeṣeṇa deśakālāvaveksya ca
—12.309.16

īdriśānaśivān ghorānācārāniha jājale
kevalācaritvāt tu nipuṇo nāvabuddhyase

—12.262.52

Simple meaning—First, time-considerations are very important, for example, dharma in Satya-yuga was different, then it changed in Treta-yuga, and then it changed again in Dvapara-yuga. Now that Kaliyuga is coming, so be sure that dharma will change again.

In fact, time, place and circumstances—all three are important; what is dharma in one situation, could be adharma in another situation.

If changes which are needed, are not made, and old practices are blindly carried on, then harmful and cruel practices (like animal sacrifice) could persist, unless educated and wise people intervene and ask the society to give up cruel practices which are no longer appropriate.

7.10. Message number eight. Give the right education to all and let this be the primary way to cultivate right values in the society (including the strengthening of fellow-feeling among all the people).

Raja-dharma's verses on this topic were presented in para 6.19 and they included a reference to the exemplary King Asvapati (although it was stressed that old ideas always need to be adjusted to changing needs). Moksa-dharma gives the same message, but makes use of Tuladhara's advice that, through education, a new value system needs to be cultivated, in which truth and non-violence get the highest priority:

नास्ति विद्यासमं चक्षुर्नास्ति सत्यसमं तपः ॥ —12.175.35
यद्भूतहितमत्यन्तमेतत् सत्यं मतं मम ॥ —12.329.13
यदा न कुरुते भावं सर्वभूतेषु पापकम् ।
कर्मणा मनसा वाचा ब्रह्म सम्पद्यते तदा ॥ —12.262.16

nāsti vidyāsamaṁ cakṣurnāsti satyasamaṁ tapaḥ

—12.175.35

yadbhūtahitamatyantametat satyaṁ mataṁ mama
—12.329.13

yadā na kurute bhāvaṁ sarvabhūteṣu pāpakam
karmaṇā manasā vācā brahma sampadyate tadā
—12.262.16

Simple meaning—Give the right education to impart the right vision (of oneness of all human beings). Through right education, give the message of truth and non-violence—truth representing the desire to do good to all, and non-violence representing the desire to be harmless, in thought, word and deed.

7.11. Message number nine. Increase food production in the country and try to make all the people healthy and prosperous.

Raja-dharma's verses on this topic were presented in para 6.20. Moksa-dharma advises that adequate food should be made available to all, by sharing, and checking that no one has too much and no one has too little—the main idea being that every one should stay healthy:

सान्त्वेनान्नप्रदानेन प्रियवादेन चाप्युत ॥ —12.297.36
संविभागं समाश्रित्य सुखी शान्तो निरामयः ॥ —12.199.123
नानाशनः स्यान्न महाशनः स्यात्
आहारप्राप्तिर्निर्वाहानुकूलम् ॥ —12.269.26

sāntvenānnapradānena privavādena cāpyuta
—12.297.36

saṁvibhāgaṁ samāśritya sukhī śānto nirāmayaḥ
—12.199.123

nānāśanaḥ syānna mahāśanaḥ syāt
āhāraprāptirnirvāhānūkulam —12.269.26

Simple meaning—Joint and co-ordinated effort is needed in the matter of food supply—the government to bring about sharing, voluntary agencies to check that no one remains hungry, and the health-care personnel to advise that, to stay healthy, no one should eat too much, and similarly no one should eat too little.

7.12. Message number ten. Take effective measures to protect the environment, for example, by planting and protecting trees.

Raja-dharma's verses on this topic were presented in para 6.21. The same message is repeated in Moksa-dharma too:

वृक्षाणामवरोपणम् ।
वन्यौषधिफलपुष्प -
मध्ये विहारसंतोष: ॥ 12.191.16

vriksāṇāmavaropaṇam
vanyauṣadhiphalapuṣpa-
madhye vihārasantoṣaḥ —12.191.16

Simple meaning—Participate in the administration's drive to plant trees. To take walks through greenery, plants and flowers is a pleasant experience for householders.

7.13. Message number eleven. Raise the status of women in the society, by empowering them through higher education.

Raja-dharma's message on this topic, as given in para 6.22, was centered on Savitri. Although Moksa-dharma has no particular woman comparable to Savitri, it does give honor to three women who achieved fame in different fields:

अत्र पिंगलया गीता गाथा: श्रूयन्ति पार्थिव ।
यथा सा कृच्छ्रकालेऽपि लेभे धर्मं सनातनम् ॥ —12.174.56
एवं सुवर्चला हृष्टा प्रोक्ता भर्त्रा यथार्थवत् ।
परिचर्यमाणा ह्यनिशं तत्त्वबुद्धिसमन्विता ॥
गार्हस्थ्यं च समाधाय गतौ जायापती परम् ॥ —12.220.1
अत्राप्युदाहरन्तीममितिहासं पुरातनम् ।
जनकस्य च संवादं सुलभायाश्च भारत ॥ —12.320.3

atra pingalayā gītā gāthāḥ śrūyanti pārthiva
yathā sā kricchrakālepi lebhe dharmaṁ sanātanam
—12.174.56

evaṁ suvarcalā hriṣṭā proktā bhartra yathārthavat
paricaryamāṇā hyaniśaṁ tattvabuddhisamanvitā
gārhasthyaṁ ca samādhāya gatau jāyāpatī param
—12.220.1

atrāpyudāharantīmamitihāsaṁ purātanam
janakasya ca saṁvādaṁ sulabhāyāśca bhārata
—12.320.3

Simple meaning—The first verse is the introductory verse to Pingala-Gita. Pingala was an ordinary woman who had fallen into bad company. But, through her own effort, she became so wise that her words are honored by Moksa-dharma as 'Pingala-Gita'.

The second verse is the summarizing verse of the story of Suvarcala. She was the daughter of sage Devala. She looked for a suitable match for herself. After a difficult search, she married the famous scholar Svetaketu who upgraded her knowledge. The couple put into practice the Vedanta philosophy in which their expertise was well-known.

The third verse is the introductory verse to the story of the saintly woman Sulabha whose knowledge of spiritual matters was comparable to that of Janaka. Moksa-dharma devotes one full chapter to Janaka-Sulabha dialogue, but we have no space here to go into detail. (Please see para 7.24).[1]

7.14. Message number twelve. Advisers should be chosen on the basis of their commitment to peace.

Raja-dharma's message on this topic, as given in para 6.23, was centered on Vidura. Moksa-dharma contains a large number of stories featuring many advisers, out of whom, we pick, for our present purpose, only two:

(i) Parasara
(ii) Tuladhara

First, the sage Parasara was the father of Vyasa. Moksa-dharma devotes nine chapters to the dialogue between Janaka and Parasara. The advice given by Parasara is honored as 'Parasara-Gita'. Here we quote only three verses therefrom:

आनृशंस्यमहिंसा चाप्रमादः संविभागिता ।
सत्यं शौचं तितिक्षा च धर्मा साधारणा नृप ॥ —12.296.23
न्यायागतं धनं चैव न्यायेनैव समर्पितम् ।
न धर्मार्थी नृशंसेन कर्मणा धनमर्जयेत् ॥ —12.292.4
परेषां यदसूयेत न तत् कुर्यात् स्वयं नरः ॥ —12.290.24

ānriśaṁsyamahimsā cāpramādaḥ saṁvibhāgitā
satyaṁ śauncaṁ titiksā ca dharmāh sādhāraṇā nripa
—12.296.23

nyāyāgataṁ dhanaṁ caiva nyāyenaiva samarpitam
na dharmārthī nriśaṁsena karmaṇā dhanamarjayet
—12.292.4

pareṣāṁ yadasūyeta na tat kuryāt svayaṁ narah
—12.290.24

Simple meaning—All members of the society should practice these virtues—absence of cruelty, non-violencc, diligence, sharing, truth, purity and tolerance.

Wealth should be acquired only by just means, and it should be spent only for lawful causes. Cruelty should be avoided in these matters.

One should not oneself do that act which, if done by someone else, would be criticized by one.

Secondly, the story of Tuladhara, which resembles the story of Vyadha (butcher) narrated by us in para 5.34. Although Tuladhara's words are not called 'Gita', they are quoted by scholars with practically the same reverence as shown to any of the Gita's.

Before we write about Tuladhara, the adviser, we must introduce the person who sought his advice, viz. Jajali, who was a yogin. Jajali was engaged in severe austerities (standing still for a long time and giving shelter to birds in his hair). Then feelings of arrogance arose in him. Soon, Jajali heard a heavenly voice, "Don't think too much of yourself. Go and see Tuladhara in Varanasi who is a more genuine follower of dharma."

After having walked for many days, Jajali reached Varanasi and went to the shop of which Tuladhara was the owner. Tuladhara said, "Honorable brahmin, I already know why you have come here. I will explain to you the real meaning of dharma."

Moksa-dharma has devoted four chapters to the dialogue between Tuladhara and Jajali, but we have space here for only two verses which summarize Tuladhara's advice:

सर्वेषां यः सुहृन्नित्यं सर्वेषां च हिते रतः ।
कर्मणा मनसा वाचा स धर्मं वेद जाजले ॥ —12.262.9
न भूतानामहिंसाया ज्यायान् धर्मोऽस्ति कश्चन ॥ —12.262.30

sarveṣām yaḥ suhrinnityaṁ sarveṣāṁ ca hite rataḥ
karmaṇā manasā vācā sa dharmaṁ veda jājale
—12.262.9
na bhūtānāmahiṁsāyā jyāyān dharmosti kaścana
—12.262.30

Simple meaning—Tuladhara said, "O Jajali, in the field of dharma, theoretical knowledge is not enough. A real knower of dharma is one who is friendly to all and who is always engaged in doing good to all, in thought, word and deed. There is no greater dharma than the practice of non-violence towards all creatures."

7.15. Message number thirteen. Since a king cannot take for granted that anti-social elements will not commit violence against the people and property of his kingdom, he should maintain self-defence capability, which depends jointly on military strength, and a feeling of unity among the people brought about by lokasamgraha-policies.

Raja-dharma's verses on this topic were presented in para 6.24. While repeating the same message, moksa-dharma adds that, if a king does not pose a threat to the neighbouring states, it is likely that they too will not pose a threat :

न जानपदिकाद् भयान्नैराश्यं कर्तुमर्हति ।
अशोचन् प्रतिकुर्वीत निर्भयेन बलेन वा ॥ —12.330.15
यस्मान्नोद्विजते भूतं जातु किंचित् कथंचन ।
सोऽभयं सर्वभूतेभ्यः सम्प्राप्नोति महामुने ॥ —12.262.30

na jānapadikād bhayānnairāśyaṁ kartumarhati
aśocan pratikurvīta niirbhayena balena vā
—12.330.15

yasmānnodvijate bhūtaṁ jātu kincit kathancana
sobhayaṁ sarvabhūtebhyaḥ samprāpnoti mahāmune
—12.262.30

Simple meaning—In order to face any threat to the state, it is important to cultivate confidence (which comes from self-defence capability), and to take steps to create an atmosphere of fearlessness. If a king does not pose a threat to the neighbouring states, it is likely that they too will not pose a threat.

7.16. Message number fourteen. Whatever disputes a king might have with the governments of other countries, he should take a firm policy decision to settle them peacefully, because wars can not provide a satisfactory solution to any dispute.

Raja-dharma's verses on this topic were presented in para 6.25. Moksa-dharma has put before kings the unique example of Vritra who changed himself, from being a peace-breaker to the glorious status of a peace-promoter (so much so that his words are honored by moksa-dharma as 'Vritra-Gita') (Please see para 5.24):

यदा मे भगवान् दृष्टो हरिर्नारायणः प्रभुः ॥ —12.297.28
तदा भूत्वा विकल्मषः तथैव भूत्वा विपाप्मा ॥ —12.280.57

yadā me bhagavān driṣṭo harirnārāyaṇaḥ prabhuḥ
—12.297.28
tadā bhūtvā vikalmaṣaḥ tathaiva bhūtvā vipāpmā
—12.280.57

Simple meaning—Shukracharya asked Vritrasura, "How is it that you have changed, from a peace-breaker to a peace-promoter?" Vritrasura replied, "When I saw Narayana (God), I became free from all my sins i.e. peace-breaking tendencies." The underlying message of moksa-dharma is that, by working for peace, a king participates in God's work.

This message was earlier given in para 5.24.

7.17. Message number fifteen. Follow the example of Indra who insisted that everyone will follow only the Commander-in-chief Kartikeya—similarly a king should not allow any private army in his kingdom.

Raja-dharma's message on this topic (given in para 6.26) was centered on Kartikeya (also known as Skanda or Kumar). The same example is quoted in moksa-dharma too:

जयार्थं सैन्यप्रमुखं कुमारमिव स्थापयेत् ।
अन्यथा राजकार्येषु दुःखं विघ्नो भयानि च ॥ 12.284.195

jayārthaṁ sainyapramukhaṁ kumāramiva sthāpayet
anyathā rājakāryeṣu duḥkhaṁ vighno bhayāni ca
—12.284.195

Simple meaning—A king can achieve success if his army is led on the pattern of Kartikeya (who was the sole commander-in-chief i.e. no private army), otherwise lots of problems will arise.

7.18. Message number sixteen. You should ensure that no donation or help or support of any kind is given to anti-social elements.

Raja-dharma's verses on this topic were presented in para 6.27. Moksa-dharma has particularly drawn attention to those who are biased against followers of other faiths, and to the great harm that can be caused due to donations given to such (anti-social) persons. (To strengthen this message, a verse from Karna-Parva has been used):

द्वेषो धर्मविशेषाणामेते वै तामसा नराः ॥ 12.313.28
ये तु पृथक्त्वमाश्रिता भूतानामहितकराः ।
न हि तेभ्यो धनं देयं शक्ये सति कथंचन ॥
पापेभ्यो हि धनं दत्तं दातारमपि पीडयेत् ॥ 8.69.64

dveṣo dharmaviśeṣāṇāmete vai tāmasā narāḥ
—12.313.28

ye tu prithaktvamāsritā bhūtānāmahitakarāh
na hi tebhyo dhanaṁ deyaṁ śakye sati kathancana
pāpebhyo hi dhanaṁ dattaṁ dātāramapi pīḍayet
—8.69.64

Simple meaning—Among anti-social elements, the worst are those who hate followers of other faiths, because they might commit violence. To such people, no donation should be given (as far as possible). In fact, those who help anti-social people, may themselves be harmed.

Additional messages of peace given to Yudhisthira in Moksa-Dharma

7.19. Moksa-dharma's style of giving messages often makes use of a story. Out of a large number of message-giving stories, we have selected five, because they obviously contain ideas having a bearing on the peace-promotion process - the underlying messages will be assigned numbers seventeen through twenty-one.

7.20. Message number seventeen. Religious leaders should not only give a free hand to the younger generation for embarking on a peace-initiative, but should also become a part of that movement.

Moksa-dharma gives this message by means of the revolutionary story of Medhavi, the son of a religious leader. The great importance attached to this story by the Mahabharata is clear from the fact that the same story is narrated twice—once in the beginning of moksa-dharma, and a second time approximately in the middle of moksa-dharma.

द्विजातेः कस्यचित् पार्थ स्वाध्यायनिरतस्य वै ।
बभूव पुत्रो मेधावी मेधावी नाम नामतः ॥ 12.175.3
मोक्षधर्मार्थकुशलो लोकतत्त्वविचक्षणः ॥ 12.175.4

dvijāteḥ kasyacit pārtha svādhyāyaniratasya vai
babhūva putro medhāvī medhāvī nāma nāmataḥ
—12.175.3
moksadharmārthakuśalo lokatattvavicakṣaṇaḥ
—12.175.4

Simple meaning—There was a brahmin who used to study ancient scriptures. He got a son whom he gave the name Medhavi—the son was intelligent (and the word 'Medhavi' also means 'intelligent'). Although the father was a traditional religious leader, he gave to his son both spiritual and secular education, of a high standard.

धीरः किंस्वित् तात कुर्यात् प्रजानन् ॥ 12.175.5

dhīraḥ kimsvit tāta kuryāt prajānan —12.175.5

Simple meaning—When Medhavi completed his education, he asked his father, "Please advise me what I should do, I want to do something 'good'."

The father said, "My dear son, we have always been doing good things, so I suggest that you continue doing the same things."

अमोघासु पतन्तीषु किं धीर इव भाषसे ॥ —12.175.7

amoghāsu patantīṣu kim dhīra iva bhāṣase
—12.175.7

Simple meaning—Medhavi said, "My respected father, how can you be so satisfied with what you have been doing? Don't you see the mess that has been created by doing things in the old way?"

अमोघाःकाः पतन्तीह किं नु भीषयसीव माम् ॥ —12.175.8

amoghāḥ kāḥ patantīha kiṁ nu bhīṣayasīva mām
—12.175.8

Simple meaning—The father said, "My dear son, why are you criticizing the old way of doing things? You are creating in me a sense of fear. Tell me what new things you want to do."

Medhavi gave a long reply, but we present here a summary in three verses:

सोऽहं ह्यहिंस्रः सत्यार्थी कामक्रोधबहिष्कृतः ।
लोकसंहारं संहर्तुं करिष्ये विशिष्टं यज्ञं ॥ —12.175.31

sohaṁ hyahiṁsraḥ satyārthī kāmakrodhabahiṣkritaḥ
lokasamhāraṁ saṁhartuṁ kariṣye viṣiṣṭaṁ yajñam
—12.175.31

Simple meaning—My movement will be based on truth and non-violence. I will get rid of all my vices like lust, anger, greed and hatred. I want to put an end to violence against mankind. In short, I want to perform a special type of yajna (to be explained in the next verse).

शान्तियज्ञरतो दान्तो ब्रह्मयज्ञे स्थितो सदा ।
वाङ्मनःकर्मयज्ञश्च भविष्यामि सर्वहितः ॥ 12.175.32

śāntiyajnarato dānto brahmayajne sthito sadā
vānmanaḥkarmayajnaśca bhaviṣyāmi sarvahitaḥ
—12.175.32

Simple meaning—The new yajna will be called 'Shanti-yajna' i.e. world peace movement. It can also be called 'brahmayajna' i.e. a movement based on oneness of all mankind. Similarly, it can be called 'vanmanahkarma-yajna' i.e. a movement to help mankind, by thought, word and deed.

नास्ति विद्यासमं चक्षुर्नास्ति सत्यसमं तपः ॥ 12.175.35

nāsti vidyāsamaṁ caksurnāsti satyasamaṁ tapaḥ
—12.175.35

Simple meaning—Medhavi added, the main emphasis of the new movement will be on education—a system of education based on truth i.e. which does not teach hatred. (This verse has been presented in para 7.10 also, but in a different context).

After listening to Medhavi, the father also joined the movement:

पुत्रस्यैतद् वचः श्रुत्वा यथाकार्षीत् पिता नृप ॥ 12.175.39

putrasyaitad vacaḥ śrutvā yathākārṣīt pitā nripa
—12.175.39

Simple meaning—Medhavi's plan was so attractive that his father too agreed to take an active part in it.

Here ends Medhāvī's story, as told in moksa-dharma. Since the concept of Shanti-yajna is so important, we want to explain it further, in the following verse (which is based on ideas contained in various parts of the Mahabharata):

शान्तिर्धर्मः शान्तिर्वार्ता शान्तिर्विद्या शान्तिः शिक्षा ।
शान्तिर्हि तदा गन्तव्या शान्तिकर्मसमाधिना ॥

śāntirdharmaḥ śāntirvārtā śāntirvidyā śāntiḥ śikṣā
śāntirhi tadā gantavyā śāntikarmasamādhinā

Simple meaning—A person can be called a performer of Shanti-yajna, if he or she considers world peace as the goal of dharma, if his or her talks are centered on world peace, if world peace is the aim of his or her education, and if he or she teaches world peace to others too—in short, if all the activities are centered on world peace. As a result of Shanti-yajna of this type, how can world peace remain out of reach?

7.21. Message number eighteen. Religious leaders should recall the dialogue between Jajali and Tuladhara, and should take part in inter-faith dialogues, enthusiastically.

The dialogue between Jajali and Tuladhara, on the topic of the real meaning of dharma, is an important part of moksa-dharma, to which four chapters have been devoted. A brief reference to it was made in para 7.14, but there the role of Tuladhara as an adviser was stressed. The point to be made here is that, this dialogue could be viewed as the Mahabharata-version of an inter-faith dialogue. Another instance of such a dialogue occurs in Vana-Parva, to which a short reference was made in para 5.34. It is obvious that the Mahabharata fully supports the concept of inter-faith dialogues.

7.22. Message number nineteen. Religious leaders should remember that their predecessors were advised by the creator to teach common people about lokasamgraha (good of all), hoping that the chain of such teaching will never be broken:

अध्यापयामास तदा लोकानां हितकाम्यया ॥ —12.348.36
त्रेतायुगादौ च ततो विवस्वान् मनवे ददौ ।
मनुश्च लोकभूत्यर्थं सुतायेक्ष्वाकवे ददौ ॥ —12.348.51
एवमेष महान् धर्मः सात्वतैर्धार्यते सदा ॥ —12.348.55
धर्मज्ञानेन चैतेन सुप्रयुक्तेन कर्मणा ।
अहिंसाधर्मयुक्तेन प्रीयते हरिरीश्वरः ॥ —12.348.56

adhyāpayāmāsa tadā lokānāṁ hitakāmyayā
—12.348.36

tretāyugādau ca tato vivasvān manave dadau
manuśca lokabhūtyarthaṁ sutāyekṣvākave dadau
—12.348.51
evameṣa mahān dharmaḥ sātvatairdhāryate sadā
—12.348.55
dharmajñānena caitena suprayuktena karmaṇā
ahiṁsādharmayuktena prīyate harirīśvaraḥ
—12.348.56

Simple meaning—In the beginning, the creator taught lokasamgraha (good of all) to the sun, who in turn passed on the teaching to Manu, and then Manu taught it to Iksvaku. In this way, the chain of teaching was kept unbroken. Generation after generation, the message of non-violence has been passed on, so that people will help one another, in thought, word and deed (rather than harm one another).

7.23. Message number twenty. Religious leaders should remember that their predecessors advised King Iksvaku to adopt the policy of Svadharma (i.e. the right to choose one's faith freely) with the hope that the same policy will be continued:

तुष्यसि त्वं स्वधर्मेण तथा तुष्टा वयं नृप ।
अन्योन्यस्यान्तरं नास्ति यदिष्टं तत् समाचर ॥ 12.199.43
नायं लोकोऽस्ति न परः स्वधर्मं चेन्न पालयेत् ॥ 12.199.61

tuṣyasi tvaṁ svadharmeṇa tathā tuṣṭā vayaṁ nripa
anyonyasyāntaraṁ nāsti yadiṣṭaṁ tat samācara
—12.199.43
nāyaṁ lokosti na paraḥ svadharmaṁ cenna pālayet
—12.199.61

Simple meaning—The guru said to Iksvaku, "O King, Svadharma policy (i.e. to give the right to everyone to choose one's faith freely) is the best policy—everyone will feel happy that way, facing no discrimination. Any departure from this policy will mean lots of problems."

7.24. Message number twenty-one. Religious leaders should remember that King Janaka welcomed Sulabha, the saintly lady, and fully supported women's right to function as a spiritual leader:

ततोऽस्याः स्वागतं कृत्वा व्यादिश्य च वरासनम् ।
पूजितां पादशौचेन वरान्नेनाप्यतर्पयत् ॥ —12.320.14
अथ भुक्तवती प्रीता राजानं मंत्रिभिर्वृतम् ।
सर्वभाष्यविदां मध्ये चोदयामास भिक्षुकी ॥ —12.320.15

tatosyāḥ svāgataṁ kritvā vyādiśya ca varāsanam
pūjitāṃ pādaśaucena varānnenāpyatarpayat
—12.320.14
atha bhuktavatī prītā rājānaṃ mantribhirvritam
sarvabhāṣyavidāṁ madhye codayāmāsa bhikṣukī
—12.320.15

Simple meaning—King Janaka welcomed the saintly lady Sulabha—when she had occupied a special seat of honor, Janaka "worshipped" her (like worshipping a goddess). After lunch, Janaka introduced Sulabha as a well-known philosopher she then addressed the assembly of great scholars. (Please see para 7.13).

Potential applications of these messages in the context of the twenty-first century

7.25. Out of all the messages that Yudhisthira received, the one given in para 7.20 has a special, potential application in the twenty-first century. In order to specify this, we first recall the message:

"Religious leaders should not only give a free hand to the younger generation for embarking on a peace-initiative, but should also become a part of that movement."

The peace-initiative referred to in this message is a translation of the Mahabharata's expression "Shanti-yajna" which has been defined in para 7.20 in the following manner (and this indicates the potential application too):

"A person can be called a performer of Shanti-yajna, if he or she considers world peace as the goal of dharma, if his or her talks are centered on world peace, if world peace is the aim of his or her education, and if he or she teaches world peace to others too—in short, if all the activities are centered on world peace. As a result of Shanti-yajna of this type, how can world peace remain out of reach?"

7.26. Another message with a great, potential application relates to education (reference paras 7.10 and 8.23, the latter is used here to strengthen the message). Again we recall the two messages:

"Religious leaders should fully support programs which seek to give the right education to all the children (i.e. boys as well as girls), and which seek to use education to cultivate right values in the society (including the strengthening of fellow-feeling among the people following different faiths)."

"The scope of educational reform programs should be widened so that they cover not only the school age children but also the adults."

By way of application of these messages, all religious schools should be told by their organizers that world peace is one of the aims of education being imparted there. Wherever the existing books contain derogatory references to any religion, those portions should either be deleted or replaced by non-derogatory write-up. In making these educational reforms, the cooperation of the adults too should be obtained.

7.27. The message on inter-faith dialogue (reference para 7.21) also has immense scope for application. Religious leaders should take part in inter-faith dialogues, enthusiastically, so that such dialogues could be held in an increasing number of places, and a written statement on "How to establish inter-religious harmony" could be produced by them.

7.28. The message on Svadharma (reference para 7.23) also offers scope for application.Religious leaders should remember that their predecessors set in motion the policy of Svadharma (i.e. the right to choose one's faith freely) with the hope that the same policy will be continued. Therefore, no support should be given to anyone who attempts to obtain conversion of faith by offering financial or other benefits.

7.29. The message on qualitative improvement of religious teaching (reference para 7.22), if properly applied, can directly promote the cause of world peace. Religious leaders should remember that their predecessors were advised by the creator to teach common people about lokasamgraha (good of all), hoping that the chain of such teaching will never be broken. Such teaching can greatly help the cause of world peace because lokasamgraha and world peace go together.

7.30. The message on raising the status of women in the society, and also on giving them the right to function as spiritual leaders (reference paras 7.13 and 7.24), if properly applied, can remove one of the obstacles to world peace. First, full support should be given to programs which seek to raise the status of women in the society, by empowering them through higher education. Secondly, religious leaders should remember that King Janaka welcomed Sulabha, the saintly lady, and fully supported women's right to function as spiritual leaders. The twenty-first century demands that the scope of women's rights should be further widened.

CHAPTER 8

Mahabharata's Messages of Peace for Consideration by Everyone Else

8.1. Chapter six gave the Mahabharata's messages of peace for consideration by Governments. Similarly, chapter seven gave the Mahabharata's messages of peace for consideration by religious leaders. The present chapter, by giving the Mahabharata's messages of peace for consideration by everyone else, will mark the end of this series.

8.2. It is useful to look at the sources from which these messages have been derived. The raja-dharma section of Shanti-Parva was the main source of the messages given in chapter six. Similarly, the moksa-dharma section of Shanti-Parva was the main source of the messages given in chapter seven. What still remained unutilized in Shanti-Parva is the apad-dharma section. Since the present chapter will give the final instalment of the messages of peace derived from Shanti-Parva, it will be appropriate to include herein the messages of peace to be derived from Anusasana-Parva too (because Bhisma's dialogue with Yudhisthira spills over from Shanti-Parva to Anusasana-Parva). This implies that the apad-dharma section of Shanti-Parva, supplemented with the whole of Anusasana-Parva, will be the source of the messages to be given in the present chapter.

8.3. Following the pattern of the preceding chapter, this chapter too will consist of three main sections:

(a) Re-affirmation, by apad-dharma (and/or Anusasana-

Parva), of the sixteen main messages, given to Yudhisthira in raja-dharma (*i.e.* the messages presented in chapter six).

(b) Additional messages of peace given to Yudhisthira in apad-dharma (as well as in Anusasana-Parva)

(c) Potential applications of these messages in the context of the twenty-first century.

Re-affirmation of the messages given in chapter six

8.4. Message number one. Give up the idea of committing suicide.

Raja-dharma's verses on this topic were quoted in para 6.12, and Moksa-dharma's verses in para 7.3. The Mahabharata attaches so much importance to this message that it is repeated in apad-dharma, and then again in Anusasana-Parva—we give below one verse each from apad-dharma and Anusasana-Parva:

आपद्काले तनुं त्यक्तुं मनो भारो विशेषतः ।
सद्बुद्धिं तु समास्थाय जीवितव्यं सदा भवेत् ॥
जीवन् पुण्यमवाप्नोति पुरुषो भद्रमश्नुते ॥ —12.141.11
अप्येवात्मवधं लोके राजंस्त्वं बहु मन्यसे ।
न हि प्रतिज्ञा या दत्ता तां प्रहातुमरिंदम ॥ —13.148.38

āpadkāle tanuṁ tyaktuṁ mano bharo viseṣataḥ
sadbuddhiṁ tu samāsthāya jīvitavyaṁ satā bhavet
jīvan punyamavāpnuti puruṣo bhadramaśnute
—12.141.101
apyevātmavadhaṁ loke rājaṁstvaṁ bahu manyase
na hi pratijnā yā dattā tāṁ prahātumarindama
—13.148.38

Simple meaning—When one is in deep distress, one feels mental pressure to end one's life. At that critical point of time, right thinking can prove to be the saviour. One whose life is thus saved, can do good deeds in due course of time and can contribute to the good of the society too

Bhisma added, "O Yudhisthira, it is not right that you keep on thinking about ending your own life. How can you do this?

You had made promises that after defeating Duryodhana, you will provide good government to the people—you cannot possibly break those promises."

8.2. Message number two. No escapism i.e. don't run away from your social responsibilities.

Raja-dharma's verses on this topic were presented in para 6.13, and moksa-dharma's verses in para 7.4. As for the previous message, this one too is considered very important by the Mahabharata, and is therefore repeated again and again. We give below two verses from apad-dharma and one from Anusasana-Parva:

सर्वभूतहितं तिष्ठ धर्मं चैव प्रतिस्मरन् ॥ —12.151.16
अनिर्वेदेन दीर्घेण निश्चयेन ध्रुवेण च ॥ —12.153.116
तथैश्वर्यं च भोगं च निष्ठा या च मनीषिता ।
सर्वं पुरुषकारेण कृतेनेहोपलभ्यते ॥ —13.6.13

sarvabhūtahitaṁ tiṣṭha dharmam caiva pratismaran
—12.151.16
anirvedena dīrghena niscayena dhruveṇa ca
—12.153.116
tathaiśvaryaṁ ca bhogaṁ ca niṣṭhā yā ca manīṣitā
sarvaṁ puruṣakāreṇa kritenehopalabhyate
—13.6.13

Simple meaning—Always remember that your duty (dharma) is to do good to all—and you should do that with firm determination and whole-hearted effort. And that will mean your own good too—it will bring prosperity, enjoyment, and right thinking to you.

8.6. Message number three. Give up gambling and let no one scoff at others as Bhima had done to Duryodhana thirteen years ago.

Raja-dharma's verses on this topic were presented in para 6.14, and moksa-dharma's verses in para 7.5. Like the earlier messages, this one too is repeated again and again. We give below one verse each from apad-dharma and Anusasana-Parva:

पानमंक्षाश्च व्यसनं परिहासो मृगया च ।
एतानि युक्त्या सेवेत प्रसंगो ह्यत्र दोषवान् ॥ —12.140.26
विशीला भिन्नमर्यादास्तथा नष्टा व्यसनेन ।
अल्पायुषो भवन्तीह नराः कुपथगामिनः ॥ —13.104.12

pānamankṣāśca vyasanaṁ parihāso mrigayā ca
etāni yuktyā seveta prasango hyatra doṣavān
—12.140.26

viśīlā bhinnamaryādāstathā naṣṭā vyasanena
alpāyuṣo bhavantīha narāḥ kupathagāminaḥ
—13.104.12

Simple meaning—Bad habits like drinking and gambling, as well as scoffing at others, and animal hunting—one might do such things occasionally, but they should not become a normal part of anyone's life. In fact, one who falls a prey to such harmful practices, is likely to lose health and die at an early age.

8.7. Message number four. The king should protect and nurture all the people living in the state, without any type of discrimination based on faith, sex, urban-rural residence, etc.

Raja-dharma's verses on this topic were presented in para 6.15, and moksa-dharma's verses in para 7.6. Apad-dharma states that, during times of distress, the role of the people in protecting the state assumes special significance, and from this angle, the no-discrimination policy of the king makes it easier for all sections of the society to forge a united front:

अन्यो धर्मः समर्थानामापत्स्वन्यश्च भारत ॥ —12.129.14
परस्परं हि संरक्षा राज्ञा राष्ट्रेण चापदि ।
नित्यमेव हि कर्तव्या एष धर्मः सनातनः ॥ —12.129.30
राजा राष्ट्रं यथाऽपत्सु सर्वोपायेन रक्षति ।
राष्ट्रेण राजा विपदि रक्षितव्यस्तथा भवेत् ॥ —12.129.31
बह्व्यः प्रतिविधातव्याः प्रज्ञा राज्ञा ततस्ततः ।
नैकशाखेन धर्मेण यत्रैषा सम्प्रवर्तते ॥ —12.142.4

anyo dharmaḥ samarthānāmāpatsvanyaśca bhārata
—12.129.14

parasparaṁ hi saṁraksā rājnā rāṣṭreṇa cāpadi
nityameva hi kartavyā eṣa dharmaḥ sanātanaḥ
—12.129.30

rājā rāṣṭraṁ yathāpatsu sarvopāyena rakṣati
rāṣṭreṇa rājā vipadi raksitavyastathā bhavet
—12.129.31

bahvyaḥ pratividhātavyāḥ prajnā rājnā tatastataḥ
naikaśākhena dharmeṇa yatraiṣā sampravartate
—12.142.4

Simple meaning—Duties of the king as well as the people, which are appropriate for times of distress, are different from those which are suitable for normal times only. During times of peace, the king bears the main responsibility for protecting the state, but during times of distress, the role of the people becomes equally important. In other words, every citizen of the state has to consider how he or she can contribute to restore peaceful conditions in the state. The no-discrimination policy of the king makes it easier for all sections of the society to forge a united front, to save the state from calamity. This provides one more justification for the king to have in his court, scholars of different faiths and opinions, and to bestow on them equal honor, at all times (i.e. not only during calamity).

8.8. Message number five. To all those who are orphans, oppressed or too weak to take care of themselves, the king should make arrangements to provide the necessary support.

Raja-dharma's verses on this topic were presented in para 6.16, and moksa-dharma's verses in para 7.7. While apad-dharma repeats the same message, Anusasana-Parva recommends a high proportion of funds to be allocated to alleviate the sufferings of poor people, during times of distress:

यत्र नास्ति ह्यार्तपीडा स राजा तीव्रशासनः ।
भीरेव नास्ति सम्बन्धो दरिद्रं यो बुभूषते ॥ —12.139.97

चतुर्धा विभजेत् कोशं धर्मभृत्यात्मकारणात् ।

आपदर्थं च नीतिज्ञो देशकालवशेन तु ॥
अनाथान् व्याधितान् वृद्धान् स्वदेशे पोषयेन्नृपः ॥ —13.145.103

yatra nāsti hyārtapīḍā sa rājā tīvraśāsanah
bhīreva nāsti sambandho daridraṁ yo bubhūṣate
—12.139.97

caturdhā vibhajet kosaṁ dharmabhrityātmakāraṇāt
āpadarthaṁ ca nītijno deśakālavaśena tu
anāthān vyādhitān vriddhhān svadeśe poṣayennripaḥ
—13.145.103

Simple meaning—Only that king can be called excellent, in whose kingdom there is no oppression, no suffering, and no atmosphere of fear, and where the poor people have a special place in the heart of the king.

The king should make arrangements to look after the orphans, the sick, and the old people-—in fact, nearly one-fourth of the state budget should be earmarked for meeting the special needs that might arise, at any time and place, in the form of any calamity.

8.9. Message number six. Give honor to old people and make special arrangements to satisfy their health and psychological needs.

Raja-dharma's verses on this topic were presented in para 6.17, and moksa-dharma's verses in para 7.8. Apad-dharma provides the rationale as to why the old people should be honored—they gave love to their children when they themselves were young, and that love can never be fully repaid (and apad-dharma explains why it is so):

त्वमद्य तु वृद्धा स्थिता पूर्वं त्वया कृता प्रीतिः ।
प्रीतिमुत्पादयेयं च प्रीतिकर्तुश्च सत्क्रियाम् ॥ —12.138.81

प्रत्युपकुर्वन् बह्वपि न भाति
पूर्वोपकारिणा तुल्यः ।
एकः करोति हि कृते
निष्कारणमेव कुरुतेऽन्यः ॥ —12.138.82

tvamadya tu vriddhā sthitā pūrvaṁ tvayā kritā prītiḥ
prītimutpādayeyaṁ ca prītikartuśca satkriyām
—12.138.81

pratyupakurvan bahavapi na bhāti
pūrvopakāriṇā tulyaḥ
ekaḥ karoti hi krite
niṣkāraṇameva kurutenyaḥ —12.138.82

Simple meaning—The young man says to his old mother, "Today you are old, but earlier you gave me lots of love. Now I want to express my love to you, but I know I can never repay your love in full—you gave your love spontaneously (without any condition), and any amount of love given by me in return can never match yours, qualitatively."

8.10. Message number seven. Whatever policy decisions a king wants to take, as a follow-up of the exemplary people of the past, he should keep in mind the importance of making the necessary adjustments or changes in the traditional concepts, corresponding to changes in time, place and circumstances.

Raja-dharma's verses on this topic were presented in para 6.18, and moksa-dharma's verses in para 7.9. Apad-dharma recommends that, instead of depending on his advisers, the king should take the lead in making adjustments and changes corresponding to changes in circumstances, and Anusasana-Parva says that such an approach can help save the state from succumbing to calamity:

स्थापयेदेव मर्यादां जनचित्तप्रसादिनीम् ।
देशकालानुकूला हि मर्यादा लोके पूजिता ॥ —12.133.13
सर्वत: सत्कृत: सद्भिर्भूतिप्रवरकारणै: ।
देशकालपात्रोचितो यो धर्मस्तं व्यवस्यति ॥ —12.132.19
एवं चरति यो राजा देशकालौ समाश्रित्य ।
तस्य राष्ट्रं धनं धर्मो यश: कीर्तिश्च वर्धते ॥ —13.145.157

sthāpayedeva maryādāṁ janacittaprasādinīm
deśakālānukūlā hi maryādā loke pūjītā
—12.133.13

sarvataḥ satkritaḥ sadbhirbhūtipravarakāraṇaiḥ
deśakālapātrocito yo dharmastaṁ vyavasyati
—12.132.19

evaṁ carati yo rājā deśakālau samāśritya
tasya rāṣṭraṁ dhanaṁ dharmo yaśaḥ kīrtiśca
vardhate —13.145.157

Simple meaning—A king's ability to make necessary adjustments to principles and practices, in the light of changes in circumstances, is very important. Only in this way can he establish socially acceptable norms of conduct, suitable for different situations. Dharma (duties) adjusted in this way can contribute to social unity and prosperity.

A state, whose king adjusts his policies to changes in time and place, achieves wealth, fame and glory, and can establish new standards of dharma acceptable to all.

8.11. Message number eight. Give the right education to all and let this be the primary way to cultivate right values in the society (including the strengthening of fellow-feeling among all the people).

Raja-dharma's verses on this topic were presented in para 6.19, and moksa-dharma's verses in para 7.10. Apad-dharma repeats the same message, but Anusasana-Parva tells a story in which the mother of a boy (who was killed by a "terrorist") puts forth a plea that right education needs to be given not only to the terrorist but also to the person who is controlling the terrorist.

First, the message from apad-dharma about the role of education. We give below one verse in which a young man is admiring his friend, and particularly his education:

सत्यमुक्तं त्वया मित्र भूतद्रोहो विगर्हितः ।
तन्मन्येऽहं तव विद्यां यस्त्वं मम हिते रतः ॥ —12.138.185

satyamuktaṁ tvayā mitra bhūtadroho vigarhitaḥ
tanmanyehaṁ tava vidyāṁ yastvaṁ mama hite rataḥ
—12.138.185

Simple meaning—My dear friend, I agree with you because you are speaking the truth viz. that friendliness with all is the most important thing in human relationships. In fact, I admire the education that you have received—it gave you the virtue to help others.

And now the famous story of Gautami from the first chapter of Anusasana-Parva. Gautami was a peace-loving woman, who was shocked to see one day that her only son has died due to snake-bite:

गौतमी नाम कौन्तेय स्थविरा शमसंयुता ।
सर्पेण दष्टं स्वं पुत्रमपश्यद्गतचेतनम् ॥ —13.1.17

gautamī nāma kaunteya sthavirā śamasaṁyutā
sarpeṇa daṣṭaṁ svaṁ putramapaśyadgatacetanam
—13.1.17

Simple meaning—Gautami, the mother of a son, wanted to live in peace, but one day she was shocked to see that her only son has died due to snake-bite.

Gautami's neighbour, Arjunaka, out of sympathy with her, caught hold of that snake and asked Gautami to authorize the killing of that snake (to take revenge for her son's death):

स चाब्रवीदयं ते स पुत्रहा पन्नगाधमः ।
ब्रूहि क्षिप्रं महाभागे वध्यतां केन हेतुना ॥ —13.1.19

sa cābravīdayaṁ te sa putrahā pannagādhamaḥ
brūhi ksipraṁ mahābhāge vadhyatāṁ kena hetunā
—13.1.19

Simple meaning—Arjunaka sympathized with Gautami, saying, "O great lady, I am sorry that your son has died, but I have caught hold of the snake who killed your son. Please authorize me to kill the snake, to take revenge for your son's death."

Arjunaka was surprised when Gautami did not say "yes"- the reason behind Gautami's reply being that she did not see any benefit which the snake's killing could give to her:

हत्वा चैनं नामृत: स्यादयं मे ।
जीवत्यस्मिन् कोऽत्यय: स्यादयं ते ॥ —13.1.23

hatvā cainaṁ nāmritaḥ syādayaṁ me
jīvatyasmin kotyayaḥ syādayaṁ te —13.1.23

Simple meaning—Gautami said, "My dear Arjunaka, thank you for your desire and effort to help me, but please tell me: Will my son become alive again when you kill this snake? Therefore I am not in favour of killing the snake. Furthermore, if the snake is not killed, will that cause any harm to you?"

Then a long discussion took place between Arjunaka and Gautami, the former arguing that the snake should be killed, while the latter suggesting that the snake should rather be reformed and advised not to bite any child in the future.

At that point, the snake spoke up and addressed Arjunaka:

को न्वर्जुनक दोषोऽत्र विद्यते मम बालिश ।
अस्वतंत्रं हि मां मृत्युर्विवशं यदचूचुदत् ॥ —13.1.35
तस्यायं वचनाद् दष्टो न कोपेन न काम्यया ।
वधमथवा शिक्षणं तत्कुरुष्व मृत्युं प्रति ॥ —13.1.36

ko nvarjunaka doṣotra vidyate mama bāliśa
asvatantraṁ he māṁ mrityurvivaśaṁ yadacūcudat
—13.1.35

tasyāyaṁ vacanād daṣṭo na kopena na kāmyayā
vadhamathavā śikṣaṇaṁ tatkuruṣva mrityuṁ prati
—13.1.36

Simple meaning—The snake said, "Dear Arjunaka, you do not know all the facts, and are therefore blaming me for the death of the boy. The fact is that I am just a tool. The plan for killing the boy was drawn up by Mrityu who used me as a tool. Personally, I had no quarrel with the boy. So Mrityu is to be blamed, not me, and whether you want to kill the culprit or educate the culprit, all that should be directed to Mrityu, not to me."

Anusasana-Parva's story does not end here. However, for

our present purpose, the above-mentioned part of the story is enough to give us the message about education, viz. that educational programs for promoting friendliness should cover not only the school-going children but also adults who are exploiting these children for their anti-social (terroristic) activities.

8.12. Message number nine. Increase food production in the country and try to make all the people healthy and prosperous.

Raja-dharma's verses on this topic were presented in para 6.20, and moksa-dharma's verses in para 7.11. An implicit message underlying these verses was that vegetarian food could help people remain healthy. Anusasana-Parva gave this message explicitly:

अधृष्यः सर्वभूतानामायुष्मान् नीरुजः सदा ।
भवत्यभक्षयन् मांसं दयावान् प्राणिनामिह ॥ —13.115.40
धन्यं यशस्यमायुष्यं स्वस्त्ययनं निरामयम् ।
मांसस्याभक्षणं प्राहुर्नियताः परमर्षयः ॥ —13.115.35
अक्रोधनः सत्यवादी भूतानामविहिंसकः ।
अनसूयुरजिह्मश्च शतं वर्षाणि जीवति ॥ —13.104.14

adhriṣyaḥ sarvabhūtānāmāyuṣmān nīrujaḥ sadā
bhavatyabhaksayan māṁsaṁ dayāvān prāṇināmiha
—13.115.40

dhanyaṁ yasasyamāyuṣyaṁ svastyayanaṁ nirāmayam
māṁsasyābhaksaṇaṁ prāhurniyatāḥ paramarṣayaḥ
—13.115.35

akrodhanaḥ satyavādī bhūtānāmavihimsakaḥ
anasūyurajihmaśca sataṁ varṣāṇi jīvati
—13.104.14

Simple meaning—One who does not eat meat, has a good chance of leading a healthy and long life. He (or she) is likely to have compassion towards all living beings - and other people too are likely to have soft feelings towards him (or her).

Ancient sages have said that a meat-less diet could give to a person prosperity, fame, long and healthy life, and happiness too.

A person who does not eat meat and practices non-violence, has a good chance of being anger-free, truthful, gentle-hearted and easy-to-live-with—such a gentle soul could live for one hundred years.

8.13. Message number ten. Take effective measures to protect the environment, for example, by planting and protecting trees.

Raja-dharma's verses on this topic were presented in para 6.21, and moksa-dharma's verses in para 7.12. While giving the same message, Anusasana-Parva has dramatized it by saying that the tree-planter should love the tree like his son :

पुष्पैः सुरगणान् वृक्षाः फलैश्चापि तथा पितॄन् ।
छायया चातिथिं तात पूजयन्ति महीरुहः ॥ —13.58.28
तस्मात् तडागे सद्वृक्षा रोप्याः श्रेयोऽर्थिना सदा ।
पुत्रवत् परिपाल्याश्च पुत्रास्ते धर्मतः स्मृताः ॥ —13.58.31

puspaiḥ suragaṇān vrikṣāḥ phalaiścāpi tathā pitrīn
chāyayā cātithiṁ tāta pūjayanti mahīruhaḥ
—13.58.28

tasmāt taḍāge sadvriksā ropyāḥ śreyorthinā sadā
putravat paripālyāśca putrāste dharmataḥ smritāḥ
—13.58.31

Simple meaning—Trees play a great role in the world — their flowers are used in temples, their fruits nourish all the people, and their shade provides shelter to travellers. Therefore, it is really a good deed for everyone to plant trees, particularly near a pond, and to love them and protect them like one's own children.

8.14. Message number eleven. Raise the status of women in the society, by empowering them through higher education.

Raja-dharma's message on this topic, as given in para 6.22,was centered on Savitri, and moksa-dharma's message (given in para 7.13) was linked with three women: Pingala,

Suvarcala, and Sulabha. Anusasana-Parva glorified Sakuntala, who, because of her wisdom and courage, successfully rose from calamity to great heights:

> नरेष्वापद्पतितेषु भार्या करोति रक्षणम् ।
> नारीष्वापद्पतितासु प्रज्ञा करोति रक्षणम् ॥
> उक्ते शकुन्तलया हि पूर्वं हितकरे वाक्ये ॥ —13.145.109
>
> *nareṣvāpadpatiteṣu bhāryā karoti raksaṇam*
> *nārīṣvāpadpatitāsu prajnā karoti raksaṇam*
> *ukte śakuntalayā hi pūrvaṁ hitakare vākye*
> —13.145.109

Simple meaning—Who protects a person, when he or she is face-to-face with calamity? Sakuntala's life provides memorable answers: (a) When a man is in calamity, his wife protects him. (b) When a woman is in calamity, her wisdom protects her.

The famous story of Sakuntala is narrated in full in the beginning of the Mahabharata. On the basis of this story, Kalidasa wrote his play which, when translated into European languages, brought universal acclaim, not only to Kalidasa but also to the entire Sanskrit literature. We give below a short summary.

Sakuntala was the daughter of the sage Visvamitra, her mother being Menaka, a heavenly nymph. But Sakuntala was brought up by the sage Kanva who found her, as an infant, on the banks of the river. Kanva gave her the name 'Sakuntala' because she was protected by birds called 'Sakunta'.

One day, King Dusyanta, during the course of a hunting expedition, visited the ashrama (hermitage) of Kanva, but the latter was not there at that time. The King fell in love with Sakuntala, so he proposed to her that they should get married according to 'Gandharva form' (i.e. mutual consent).But Sakuntala placed a condition, viz. that if I give birth to a son, then he will succeed you on the throne.

Dusyanta accepted Sakuntala's condition, stayed with her at the ashrama for a while, and then returned to his kingdom. Kanva gave his blessings to Sakuntala and continued to look after her as also the son to whom she gave birth. In fact, the little boy spent the first six years of his life in Kanva's ashrama—the name 'Sarva-damana'(meaning one who could control all animals) was given to him.

Sakuntala's greatness was particularly brought to light when she and her six-year old son went to Dusyanta and, seeing that the King pretended not to remember his visit to Kanva's ashrama, she had to plead forcefully for the truth to be honored. B.A. van Nooten says, "Sakuntala, looking the King straight in the face, burst forth in an impassioned speech, one of the finest in the epic."[1]

Sakuntala's statement received incontrovertible support from a heavenly voice which convinced the King as well as all others. Then Dusyanta bestowed full honors on Sakuntala and showered paternal affection on the little boy who was given a new name 'Bharata' as advised by the heavenly voice. The King told Sakuntala that he had never forgotten her—he had only wanted the common people to hear the full story through the heavenly voice so that they too are convinced about the legitimacy of their son.

The qualities, which Bharata had acquired at Kanva's ashrama, were further developed under the parental care of Sakuntala and Dusyanta. In due course of time, Bharata succeeded Dusyanta as a King but surpassed him—and all other ancient rulers too—so much so that the Sanskrit name of India viz. "Bharata-varsa" is derived from him. Sakuntala has been duly recognized as the mother who contributed so much to the building of Bharata's character.

8.15. Message number twelve. Advisers should be chosen on the basis of their commitment to peace.

Raja-dharma's message on this topic, as given in para 6.23, was centered on Vidura, and moksa-dharma's message (given in para 7.14) was linked with two advisers viz. Parasara and Tuladhara. Apad-dharma and Anusasana-Parva have put forth an idea that, in times of crisis, if a human adviser is not in sight, perhaps an animal or bird or reptile or fish, could give the right advice. A notable example of this has been given in para 8.11 where a snake spoke words of wisdom relating to education. In fact, moksa-dharma too made a little use of this technique (reference para 7.3) when a jackal spoke effectively against suicide. Also, towards the end of the Mahabharata, the message "Don't make anyone unhappy, for the sake of your own happiness" is given by using a dog as a silent but important actor in a dramatic situation. We have summarized this two-track approach of the Mahabharata (using an animal as a speaker or as a tool) in the following verse:

आपद्काले तु जन्तुभिः देयः सद्धर्मसंदेशः ।
ज्ञेयो विद्वद्भिः ह्यथवा जन्तुः निमित्तरूपेण ॥

āpadkāle tu jantubhiḥ deyaḥ saddharmasandesaḥ
jneyo vidvadbhiḥ hyathavā jantuḥ nimittarūpeṇa

Simple meaning—Scholars can recognize if, at a critical point of time, an animal speaks words of wisdom. Similarly, they can also recognize if the author of the Mahabharata uses an animal as a tool, for giving a message of peace.

The most famous example of the use of the second variant (viz. using a dog as a tool, for giving an important message) occurs towards the end of the Mahabharata. We give below a short summary.

When Yudhisthira attained the age of retirement, he installed Arjuna's grandson Pariksita on the throne. The five Pandava brothers, accompanied by Draupadi, then started the final journey on foot, to high mountains leading to heaven's entrance. With a view to testing Yudhisthira's adherence to the subtle principles of righteousness, the Lord of Dharma assumed the form of a dog who became the seventh member of the walking team.

Shortly before Yudhisthira and the dog approached the entrance to heaven, Draupadi fell down, and thereafter Sahadeva, Nakula, and Arjuna fell down too, in that order, and finally Bhima also fell down. Each time, Bhima asked Yudhisthira why the particular person fell, and Yudhisthira gave him a reply. Such exchange of words between the two brothers occurred five times. Yudhisthira's replies help us understand what dharma is, or rather what adharma (violation of dharma) is. Having replied to Bhima's last question, Yudhisthira walked on. At this point he had only one companion,viz. the dog that walked behind him.

At the entrance to heaven, Indra (the chief of heaven) greeted Yudhisthira and said, "Welcome, righteous soul, please ascend this chariot so that I can take you to heaven."

Yudhisthira said, "O chief of heaven, I do not want to go to heaven alone. So, if you want to take me to heaven, please arrange that my brothers and wife, who have fallen on the way, may accompany me."

When Indra said that the brothers and wife are already in heaven, Yudhisthira put one more condition, "This dog has been walking with me, so please allow him to accompany me to heaven."

At this point, Indra expressed his inability to agree, saying that, according to rules, dogs are not allowed entry into heaven.

Then Yudhisthira announced his decision:

तस्मान्नाहं जातु कथंचनाद्य
त्यक्ष्याम्येनं स्वसुखार्थी महेन्द्र ॥ —17.3.11

tasmānnāhaṁ jātu kathancanādya
tyaksyāmyenaṁ svasukhārthī mahendra —17.3.11

Simple meaning—"O chief of heaven, please excuse me for not accepting your invitation to enter heaven, because for the sake of my own happiness, I will never abandon this dog."

Suddenly, the dog became transformed into his real form (i.e. The Lord of Dharma), who then admired Yudhisthira, "You renounced Indra's chariot, but not the dog. Hence there is no one in heaven who might be equal to you."

8.16. Message number thirteen. Since a king cannot take for granted that anti-social elements will not commit violence against the people and property of his kingdom, he should maintain self-defence capability, which depends jointly on military strength, and a feeling of unity among the people brought about by lokasamgraha-policies.

Raja-dharma's verses on this topic were presented in para 6.24, and moksa-dharma's verses in para 7.15. The same message is repeated, in a summarized form, in Anusasana-Parva:

सर्वोद्योगं स्वयं कुर्याद् दुर्गादिषु सदा नृषु ।
देशवृद्धिकरान् भृत्यानप्रमादेन कारयेत् ॥ —13.145.93

sarvodyogaṁ svayaṁ kuryād durgādiṣu sadā nriṣu
deśavriddhikarān bhrityānapramādena kārayet
—13.145.93

Simple meaning—The king should take special interest in matters of self-defence preparedness. He should also direct his administration to give high priority to build up socio-economic strength, and to consider it as a tool for self-defence.

8.17. Message number fourteen. Whatever disputes a king might have with the governments of other countries, he should take a firm policy decision to settle them peacefully, because wars can not provide a satisfactory solution to any dispute.

Raja-dharma's verses on this topic were presented in para 6.25, and moksa-dharma's verses in para 7.16. Apad-dharma recalls that raja-dharma had advised kings to lay down a clear policy for avoiding war, and also to have ministers specially trained to implement this policy successfully. Apad-dharma then adds that these suggestions are particularly needed for tackling critical situations:

वर्जनीयं सदा युद्धमेतां नीतिं समाश्रित्य ॥ —12.69.23
शान्तिज्ञानविशारदाः सन्मतिदाश्च मंत्रिणः ॥ —12.115.17
राजधर्मेण वांछिता ह्यापद्काले विशेषतः ॥ —12.130.2

varjanīyaṁ sadā yuddhametāṁ nītiṁ samāśritya
—12.69.23

śāntijnānaviśāradāḥ sanmatidāśca mantriṇaḥ

—12.115.17

rājadharmeṇa vānchitā hyāpadkāle viśeṣataḥ

—12.130.20

Simple meaning—The first two verses occur originally in raja-dharma and they say two things: (a) A king should lay down a clear policy that he wants to avoid war. (b) The king should have ministers specially trained to implement this policy successfully. The third verse then emphasizes that these suggestions, which are useful for normal times, are particularly useful for tackling critical situations.

Anusasana-Parva has also suggested that a king should avoid war as far as possible:

प्रायशो वर्जयेद् युद्धं प्रजा: सर्वत्र पालयेत् ।
व्यसनेभ्यो बलं रक्षेन्नयतो व्ययतोऽपि वा ॥ —13.145.108

prāyaśo varjayed yuddhaṁ prajāḥ sarvatra pālayet
vyasanebhyo balaṁ rakṣennayato vyayatopi vā

—13.145.108

Simple meaning—A king should avoid war as far as possible, through diplomatic effort. All available resources should be spent on developmental activities, benefitting all the people. Special precaution should be taken that the defence personnel perform only the tasks assigned to them by the civilian authorities, and that they (i.e. defence personnel) stay away from bad habits (like drinking and misconduct or interference in policy matters).

8.18. Message number fifteen. A king should follow the example of Indra who insisted that everyone will follow only the commander-in-chief Kartikeya—similarly a king should not allow any private army in his kingdom.

Raja-dharma's verses on this topic were presented in para 6.26, and moksa-dharma's verse in para 7.17. Anusasana-Parva repeats the same message:

प्रजानां रक्षणार्थाय प्रजाहितकरो भवेत्।
नृपो जनपदं रक्षेत् स्वसैन्येनैव नान्यथा ॥
स्वसैन्यं तु परित्यज्य यो युद्धेत् स भयावहः ॥ —13.145.84

prajānāṁ rakṣaṇārthāya prajāhitakaro bhavet
nripo janapadaṁ rakset svasainyenaiva nānyathā
svasainyaṁ tu parityajya yo yuddhet sa bhayāvahaḥ
—13.145.84

Simple meaning—A king should utilize his army for purposes of protecting all the people of the state. He should also ensure that no one leaves the state's army with a view to building up any private army.

8.19. Message number sixteen. You should ensure that no donation or help or support of any kind is given to anti-social elements.

Raja-dharma's verses on this topic were presented in para 6.27, and moksa-dharma's verses in para 7.18. Anusasana-Parva repeats the same message:

ये परस्वापहर्तारः परस्वानां च नाशकाः ।
सूचकाश्च परेषां ये ते वै कुपात्रा निश्चिताः ॥ —13.23.62

ye parasvāpahartāraḥ parasvānāṁ ca nāśakāḥ
sūcakāśca pareṣāṁ ye te vai kupātrā niścitāḥ
—13.23.62

Simple meaning—Those who kill others or deprive others of their wealth or hate others—such anti-social people, definitely do not deserve any donation or help.

Additional messages of peace given to Yudhisthira in apad-dharma and Anusasana-Parva

8.20. We will follow in this section the same pattern as was adopted in the preceding chapter, viz. to select a narration which gives a message of peace, directly or indirectly. Seven such messages are given below, and they will be assigned numbers twenty-two through twenty-eight (taking into account messages 17-21 presented in the preceding chapter).

8.21. Message number twenty-two. Following the advice of apad-dharma, ordinary individuals should be inspired to consider how, in times of crisis, they could help their government, although, in times of peace, the state might be supposed to take the lead:

अन्यो धर्मः समस्थस्य विषमस्थस्य चापरः ।
आपदस्तु कथं शक्याः परिपाठेन वेदितुम् ॥ —12.260.4

anyo dharmaḥ samasthasya viṣamasthasya cāparaḥ
āpadastu kathaṁ śakyāh paripāthena veditum

—12.260.4

Simple meaning—Duties of citizens vary, depending on whether they are living in times of peace or in times of crisis. Written texts mostly advise about times of peace, when the government is supposed to take the lead. However, in times of crisis, it becomes the duty of the citizens to help the government, and to take the initiative for tiding over the crisis. This message is similar to the one given in para 5.37.

8.22. Message number twenty-three. Anusasana-Parva has suggested that, since women will benefit the most, from world peace, they should take the initiative to create public opinion in favour of peace. (The word used in the text is 'Shantirishta', and this needs to be linked to Shanti-yajna which was explained in para 7.20):

पुरं जनपदं नारीः शान्तिरिष्टेन पोषयेत् ।
पुत्रान् पौत्रान् पतींश्चैव बांधवान् शिक्षकांस्तथा ॥ 13.9.23

puraṁ janapadaṁ nārīḥ śāntiriṣṭena poṣayet
putrān pautrān patīṁscaiva bāndhavān
śikṣakāṁstathā —13.9.23

Simple meaning—When peace is established in a state, the women will feel benefitted the most, because their husbands, brothers, sons and grandsons as well as the teachers of their children, usually bear the brunt of war. (The word 'Shantirishta' means 'benefits caused by peace"- if linked with para 7.20, the underlying message is that, the potential beneficiaries should take the initiative for Shanti-yajna).

8.23. Message number twenty-four. Anusasana-Parva has used the story of Gautami to convey the message that the scope of educational reform programs should be widened so that they cover not only the school-age children but also the adults.

The story of Gautami has been told in para 8.11, but the main emphasis there was on giving the right education to children. The additional message derived from this story is that the adults too should receive the right education. (Please see para 7.26).

8.24. Message number twenty-five. Anusasana-Parva has warned against the practice of offering financial rewards for faith conversion, arguing that similar benefits are attainable, without any conversion. (The use of force for obtaining faith conversion is condemnable on several grounds):

स्वधर्मशीलेषु च धर्मवित्सु
वृद्धोपसेवानिरते च दान्ते ।
कृतात्मनि क्षान्तिपरे समर्थे
वसामि नित्यं सुभगे प्रगल्भे ॥ —13.11.10
भावेन यस्मिन् निवसामि पुंसि
स वर्धते धर्मयशोऽर्थकामैः ॥ —13.11.21

svadharmaśīleṣu ca dharmavitsu
vriddhopasevānirate ca dānte
kritātmani kṣāntipare samarthe
vasāmi nityaṁ subhage pragalbhe —13.11.10
bhāvena yasmin nivasāmi puṁsi
sa vardhate dharmayaśorthakāmaih —13.11.21

Simple meaning—Laksmi, the goddess of prosperity, says, "A person following sva-dharma need not be misled if any one offers him money for getting converted, because even without conversion, he will have plenty of money. Of course, I expect him to be virtuous, devoted to the service of the elders, self-disciplined, and forgiving."

8.25. Message number twenty-six. Anusasana-Parva has

recommended that mental attitudes of people can be oriented to non-killing, if they give up meat-eating.

Anusasana Parva recommends a vegetarian diet, on two main grounds, viz. philosophical grounds, and health grounds. By philosophical grounds, is meant the characterization of vegetarian diet as an essential component of non-violence, the other three components being: not to harm any one, by thought, word, and deed. Secondly, by health grounds, is meant the likelihood of achieving good health and long life, by means of vegetarian food. This aspect (i.e. health) has already been covered in para 8.12. So the additional message given here is the advice regarding vegetarian diet on philosophical grounds—of course, health benefits will be received too, but the emphasis is on developing a non-killing mentality :

हिंसां तु मनसा त्यक्त्वा तथा वाचाथ कर्मणा ।
न भक्षयति यो मांसमहिंसकः स उच्यते ॥ —13.114.8
चतुर्विधेयं निर्दिष्टा ह्यहिंसा ब्रह्मवादिभिः ।
एकैकतोऽपि विभ्रष्टा न भवत्यरिसूदन ॥ —13.114.4
रूपमव्यंगतामायुः सद्बुद्धिमहिंसां स्मृतिम् ।
प्राप्तुकामैर्नरैर्मांसं वर्जितं वै महात्मभिः ॥ —13.115.6

himsām tu manasā tyaktvā tathā vācātha karmaṇā
na bhakṣayati yo māṁsamahiṁsakaḥ sa ucyate
—13.114.8
caturvidheyaṁ nirdiṣṭā hyahimsā brahmavādibhiḥ
ekaikatopi vibhraṣṭā na bhavatyarisūdana
—13.114.4
rūpamavyangatāmāyuḥ sadbuddhimahimsāṁ smritim
prāptukāmairnarairmāṁsaṁ varjitam vai mahātmabhiḥ —13.115.6

Simple meaning—A three-dimensional concept of non-violence visualizes the desire not to harm anyone, by thought, word, or deed. To this, is added the fourth dimension, viz. meat-less diet. Then it is called 'non-violence'. In fact, complete non-violence means a combination of all these four—if any one of the four is absent, then we have incomplete non-violence

Those who give up meat-eating (as a part of their non-violent philosophy) are likely to develop a non-killing mentality, and also enjoy a healthy and beautiful body, long life and good memory.

8.26. Message number twenty-seven. Anusasana-Parva has told a story in which a monster (initially bent on killing) was won over by non-violence, suggesting that such stories might generate people's interest in non-violence.

This is an important story giving a message of peace. However, because of limited space, we need to present below the story in brief only.

कश्चिद् वाग्बुद्धिसम्पन्नो ब्राह्मणो विजने वने ।
गृहीतः कृच्छ्रमापन्नो रक्षसा भक्षयिष्यता ॥ —13.124.5

kaścid vāgbuddhisampanno brāhmaṇo vijane vane
grihītaḥ kricchramāpanno raksasā bhakṣayiṣyatā
—13.124.5

Simple meaning—A certain brahmin, imbued with eloquence as well as intelligence, fell into distress, because he was seized in a lone forest by a monster who wished to feed on him.

स बुद्धिश्रुतिसम्पन्नस्तं दृष्ट्वातीव भीषणम् ।
सामैवास्मिन् प्रयुयुजे न मुमोह न विव्यथे ॥ —13.124.6

sa buddhiśrutisampannastaṁ driṣṭvātīva bhiṣaṇam
sāmaivāsmin prayuyuje na mumoha na vivyathe
—13.124.6

Simple meaning—Since the brahmin was learned and wise, he kept his calm. Without allowing himself to be stupefied at the sight of that terrible cannibal, he resolved to apply the method of non-violence.

रक्षस्तु वाचं सम्पूज्य प्रश्नं पप्रच्छ तं द्विजम् ।
मोक्ष्यसे ब्रूहि मे प्रश्नं केनास्मि हरिणः कृशः ॥ —13.124.7

raksastu vācaṁ sampūjya prasnaṁ papraccha taṁ dvijam
mokṣyase brūhi me prasnaṁ kenāsmi hariṇaḥ krisaḥ —13.124.7

Simple meaning—The monster was impressed by the brahmin's sweet words and calm face. He did not carry out his initial intention of killing the brahmin. Rather he offered to give him a chance by saying, "I shall release you if you give me a satisfactory reply to my question: Why am I pale and lean?"

मुहूर्तमथ संचिन्त्य ब्राह्मणस्तस्य रक्षसः।
आभिर्गाथाभिरव्यग्नः प्रश्नं प्रतिजगाद ह॥ —13.124.8

muhūrtamatha sancintye brāhmaṇastasya rakṣasaḥ
ābhirgāthābhiravyagnaḥ praśnaṁ pratijagāde ha
—13.124.8

Simple meaning—After reflecting for a while, the brahmin calmly accepted the conditional offer of the monster and proceeded to give his reply to the monster's question.

The brahmin offered thirty different possibilities as to why the monster was pale and lean—but we give below only four of them:

क्लिश्यमानान् विमार्गेषु कामक्रोधावृतात्मनः।
मन्ये त्वं ध्यायसि जनांस्तेनासि हरिणः कृशः॥ 13.124.15

kliśyamānān vimārgeṣu kāmakrodhāvritātmanaḥ
manye tvaṁ dhyāyasi janāṁstenāsi hariṇaḥ kriśaḥ
—13.124.15

Simple meaning—Perhaps you feel sorry for those persons who follow a wrong path under the influence of lust and anger, and who therefore suffer misery in this world. Such sympathy for incurable sinners makes you pale and lean.

नूनमर्थवतां मध्ये तव वाक्यमनुत्तमम्।
न भाति कालेऽभिहितं तेनासि हरिणः कृशः॥ 13.124.23

nūnamarthavatāṁ madhye tava vākyamanuttamam
na bhāti kālebhihitaṁ tenāsi hariṇaḥ kriśaḥ
—13.124.23

Simple meaning—While in the company of rich persons, you may find that, howsoever wisely you speak, they criticize your words as being unwise and inappropriate to the occasion. Such criticism makes you pale and lean.

परस्परविरुद्धानां प्रियं नूनं चिकीर्षसि ।
सुहृदामुपरोधेन तेनासि हरिणः कृशः ॥ —13.124.37

parasparaviruddhānāṁ priyaṁ nūnaṁ ciikīrṣasi
suhridāmuparodhena tenāsi hariṇaḥ kriśaḥ
—13.124.37

Simple meaning—Desirous of reforming your friends, who fight among themselves, you try to bring them together, for their good, but probably you are worried about the degree of success. Such worry makes you pale and lean.

श्रोत्रियांश्च विकर्मस्थान् प्राज्ञांश्चाप्यजितेन्द्रियान् ।
मन्येऽनुध्यायसि जनांस्तेनासि हरिणः कृशः ॥ —13.124.38

śrotriyāṁsca vikarmasthān prājnāṁscapyajitendriyān
manyenudhyāyasi janāṁstenāsi hariṇaḥ kriśaḥ
—13.124.38

Simple meaning—Desirous of reforming important persons, you try to help, for example, you try that Vedic scholars should get away from improper acts, and other learned persons should similarly get out of the slavery of their senses, but probably you are worried about the degree of success. Such worry makes you pale and lean.

Now the final verse of the story aimed at illustrating the victory of non-violence:

एवं सम्पूजितं रक्षो विप्रं तं प्रत्यपूजयत् ।
सखायमकरोच्चैनं संयोज्यार्थैर्मुमोच ह ॥ —13.124.39

evaṁ sampūjitaṁ rakso vipraṁ taṁ pratyapūjayat
sakhāyamakaroccainaṁ saṁyojyārthairmumoca ha
—13.124.39

Simple meaning—After getting such a fine and respectful reply to his question, the monster too adopted a worshipful attitude, viz. that he made the brahmin his friend, and (instead of eating him up), gave him a nice gift of money, and let him off to freedom.

8.27. Message number twenty-eight. Bhisma paid tribute to persons who had told him the important stories of Gautami, Medhavi and other peace-promoting individuals—the underlying message being that writers and journalists (or media people in general) should record and popularize the contributions that ordinary persons are making all the time to the cause of world peace, in different countries.

The story of Gautami has been presented in para 8.11, and the story of Medhavi in para 7.20. These are two of the most important stories through which the contribution of ordinary individuals of ancient times, to the cause of peace, has been made available to us. Inspired by this, all categories of media people, while reporting about peace breakers, should, at the same time, report about peace-promoters too.

Potential applications of these messages in the context of the twenty-first century

8.28. Out of all the messages that Yudhisthira received, the one given in para 8.21 (which is similar to the message of para 5.37) has a special, potential application in the twenty-first century. In order to specify this, we first recall and rephrase the message:

"United Nations can draw a lesson from the Mahabharata and try to make the peace process a mass movement, so that all the people of the world can make their contribution to world peace."

One way of achieving this goal could be that UN should designate 24th October as 'World Peace Day', and obtain the approval of all the governments to the effect that 'World Peace Day' will be celebrated in all the countries, by educational institutions (with full participation of students), as well as by women's organizations and other non-governmental groups.

During the rest of the year too, different types of peaceful functions (as determined by local people), in support of world peace, should be held. The Mahabharata's expression for peace-initiative taken by common people is 'Shanti-yajna' which is a significant word implying strong commitment and participation of all (reference para 7.20).

8.29. Corresponding to the 'Shanti-yajna'-based message, para 8.22 presents 'Shanti-rista'-based message, which also has a vast potential. The word 'Shanti-rista' means benefits caused by peace. When peace is established, the women will feel benefitted the most, because their husbands, brothers, sons and grandsons as well as the teachers of their children, usually bear the brunt of war. This idea can be generalized, to cover all categories of war-ravaged sections of the society—all of them should be given full support when they try to mould public opinion in favour of world peace.

8.30. The famous story of Gautami (reference paras 8.11 and 8.23) sends an important message to educational authorities:

The scope of educational reform programs should be widened so that they cover not only the school-age children but also the adults.

Practical applications of Gautami's story, like those of Medhavi's story (reference para 7.20), have a direct impact on the peace process. (Please see para 7.26).

8.31. The message on qualitative improvement of food, if applied on a long-term basis, can orient the mental attitudes of people to non-killing. Therefore, vegetarian societies and other groups collaborating with them, should be given full freedom to carry on their publicity against meat-eating (reference para 8.25).

8.32. Messages contained in paras 8.26 and 8.27 open up a vast field of application by writers and journalists (or media people in general). They should record and popularize the contributions that ordinary persons (men, women and children) are making all the time to the cause of world peace, in different parts of the world.

CHAPTER 9

Summary of the Peace Messages and Concluding Remarks

9.1. Having given nearly one hundred messages of peace, in chapters two through eight, we now present, in the first part of this chapter, a consolidated summary of those messages, classified in terms of the following five categories:

Category one: Messages to be considered by common people of the world and NGO's.

Category two: Messages to be considered by religious leaders of different faiths.

Category three: Messages to be considered by governments of different countries.

Category four: Messages to be considered by UNESCO.

Category five: Messages to be considered by the United Nations.

The second part of this chapter will then look at ways of achieving a purposeful, goal-oriented follow-up of the messages contained in this book—the goal being world peace.

9.2. Although four sources (viz. Vedas, Upanisads, Bhagavad-Gita, and Mahabharata) have been selectively used by us to derive the various messages, the Mahabharata has been taken to be the arbiter in the sense that it represents what appears to us to be feasible in the twenty-first century. We urge the readers to view the messages that are summarized here, as essentially non-denominational in character. No criticism of any faith or government is intended here. Furthermore, if the readers would like to modify some of the messages, that by itself might not take the messages beyond the acceptability limits of the Mahabharata, since flexibility is one of its main features.

Category one: Messages to be considered by common people of the world and NGO's

9.3. We have assigned category one to these messages because one of our main recommendations that will interest common people, is that world peace needs to be made a mass movement, in order to accelerate the possible rate of progress towards the goal of peace.

This recommendation, and twenty-four other messages (mainly from chapter eight) are listed in a summarized form below - the underlying idea being that world peace promotion policies are more likely to be followed by those governments which are democratic and which carry on all round developmental activities for all the people of their own country to begin with:

(i) Common people of the world should take an active interest in removing the obstacles to world peace (caused by anti-social elements) and they (i.e. common people) should not leave this important matter to be tackled only by UN or their governments or religious leaders. In order to give a concrete shape to their interest in establishing world peace, organizations representing every section of the society, in every country, should specifically declare world peace promotion as one of their objectives. It may be helpful to prepare an illustrative list of organizations that should get actively involved in this noble cause— educational and training institutions, health promoting organizations, yoga and meditation groups, veterans groups, all types of media, movie producers and distributors, sports groups, senior citizens, women's organizations, children's welfare groups, student exchange organizations, people-to-people contact groups, vegetarian food promotion clubs, ahimsa-based organizations, environmental protection groups, and so on. Of course, it is upto each organization to decide what it wants to do.

(ii) No support should be given to anyone who may be planning to commit suicide. (This message was the first one given in Shanti-Parva, hence it has been given priority here. For the twenty-first century, this message means that suicide bombers are not to be given any support). (For details, please see para 8.4).

(iii) No support should be given to anyone who may be planning to ignore his or her social responsibilities (which include the maintenance of world peace).

(iv) No support should be given to anyone who scoffs at other people's faith (through cartoons, for example).

(v) No support should be given to discrimination based on faith, sex, race, colour, language, country of residence, etc.

(vi) Full support should be given to programs which are meant to help those who are orphans, oppressed, or too weak to take care of themselves. (Sympathy for such persons may create the desire to avoid violence or war, which aggravates this type of problems).

(vii) Full support should be given to programs which are meant to honor old people or which seek to make special arrangements to satisfy their health and psychological needs.

(viii) Full support should be given to programs which seek to make necessary adjustments or changes in traditional concepts, to keep pace with changes in time, place and circumstances. (To put an end to historical animosities is one such program).

(ix) Full support should be given to programs which seek to give the right education to all the children (i.e. boys as well as girls), and which seek to use education to cultivate right values in the society (including the strengthening of fellow-feeling among the people following different faiths).

(x) The scope of educational reform programs should be widened so that they cover not only the school-age children but also the adults. (For more details on this special message, please see para 8.11).

(xi) Full support should be given to programs which seek to increase food production in the country, as also to increase employment opportunities in socially useful jobs, and which seek to make all the people healthy and prosperous. (Increasing employment opportunities in the military for aggressive purposes is not covered in this message).

(xii) Full support should be given to programs which seek to protect the environment, for example, by planting and protecting trees. (Damage to environment is particularly severe due to war).

(xiii) Full support should be given to programs which seek to raise the status of women in the society, by empowering them through higher education. (For more details on this special message, please see para 8.14).

(xiv) At the time of elections, or when selection is made for filling important positions, only those candidates should be supported who are enthusiastic about promoting world peace.

(xv) Full support should be given to government programs which seek to maintain self-defence capability—keeping in mind the fact that such capability depends jointly on military strength, and a feeling of unity among the people brought about by no-discrimination policies of the government. (For more details on this special message, please see para 8.16).

(xvi) Full support should be given to the following: Whatever disputes a country might have with the governments of other countries, its government should take a firm policy decision to settle them peacefully, because wars cannot provide a satisfactory solution to any dispute. (For more details on this special message, please see para 8.17).

(xvii) No support should be given to the idea of anyone having a private army, because all military should be under the direct control of the government. (For more details on this special message, please see para 8.18).

(xviii) No donation or help or support of any kind should be given to anti-social elements which arc likcly to disturb world peace. (For details please see para 8.19).

(xix) Full support should be given to war-ravaged sections of the society in their attempt to mould public opinion in favour of world peace. (For more details on this special message, please see para 8.22).

(xx) No support should be given to anyone who attempts to obtain conversion of faith by offering financial or other benefit.

(xxi) Vegetarian societies and other groups collaborating with them, should be given full freedom to carry on their publicity against meat-eating. (For more details on this special message, please see para 8.25).

(xxii) Non-violent activists should be given full freedom to carry on their publicity in support of world peace.

(xxiii) Writers and journalists (or media people in general) should record and popularize the contributions that ordinary persons (men, women and children) are making all the time to the cause of world peace, in different countries. (For more details on this special message, please see paras 8.26 and 8.27).

(xxiv) Full support should be given (in countries where this message is applicable), to any proposal which seeks to replace, by peaceful means, a dictatorial form of government, by a democratic set-up, because such a change would be conducive to world peace. (For more details on this special message, please see para 5.36).

(xxv) Full support should be given to any proposal which seeks to establish, by peaceful means, a secular democratic set-up in any country (where this message is applicable), because a theocratic set-up at home is less likely to promote world peace, as compared to a secular set up. (For more details on this special message, please see paras 3.15 and 5.23).

Category two: Messages to be considered by religious leaders of different faiths

9.4. Before we summarize the messages of this category, we want to draw attention to our main recommendation in regard to religious leaders of different faiths, viz. that they should declare world peace to be one of the goals of their respective faith. This recommendation, and twenty-eight other messages (mainly from chapter seven) are listed here in a summarized form. Most of the messages are similar to the ones listed under category one, because this is what the Mahabharata has done (Shanti-Parva has repeated the same messages three times). We have included more messages in category two, than in the other categories—the underlying idea being that, in the twenty-first century, the role of religious leaders in establishing world peace will be particularly important:

(i) Religious leaders of different faiths can really help by declaring world peace to be one of the goals of their respective faith, and by taking five supportive steps to strengthen this declaration:

(a) Religious leaders of every faith should prepare written statements in different languages, explaining how they can contribute to world peace.

(b) Religious leaders of every faith should declare that those who are breaking peace in the name of their faith are acting against the official policy of that faith.

(c) Written instructions should be sent to all the places of worship of every faith, explaining how they should spread the message of world peace, in their area of operation.

(d) Written instructions should be sent to the field staff of every faith (other than those covered by places of worship), explaining how they should spread the message of world peace at the local level.

(e) All religious schools should be told by their organizers that world peace is one of the aims of education being imparted there.

(ii) No religious sanction should be given to anyone who may be planning to commit suicide. (Potential suicide bombers need to be dissuaded on two grounds, viz. that killing innocent people is anti-religion, and that committing suicide is also anti-religion—and such advice can best be given by religious leaders).

(iii) No support should be given to any one who may be planning to ignore his or her social responsibilities (which include the maintenance of world peace).

(iv) No support should be given to any one who scoffs at other people's faith (through cartoons, for example).

(v) No support should be given to discrimination based on faith, sex, race, colour, language, country of residence, etc.

(vi) Full support should be given to programs which are meant to help those who are orphans, oppressed, or too weak to take care of themselves. (Sympathy for such persons may create the desire to avoid violence or war, which aggravates this type of problems).

(vii) Full support should be given to programs which are meant to honor old people or which seek to make special arrangements to satisfy their health and psychological needs.

(viii) Full support should be given to programs which seek to make necessary adjustments or changes in traditional concepts, to keep pace with changes in time, place and circumstances. (To put an end to historical animosities is one such program).

(ix) Full support should be given to programs which seek to give the right education to all the children (i.e. boys as well as girls), and which seek to use education to cultivate right values in the society (including the strengthening of fellow-feeling among the people following different faiths). Wherever the existing books contain derogatory references to any religion, those portions should either be deleted or replaced by non-derogatory write-up.

(x) The scope of educational reform programs should be widened so that they cover not only the school age children but also the adults. (For more details on this special message, please see para 8.11).

(xi) Full support should be given to programs which seek to increase food production in the country, as also to increase employment opportunities in socially useful jobs, and which seek to make all the people healthy and prosperous. (Increasing employment opportunities in the military for aggressive purposes is not covered in this message).

(xii) Full support should be given to programs which seek to protect the environment, for example, by planting and protecting trees. (Damage to environment is particularly severe due to war).

(xiii) Full support should be given to programs which seek to raise the status of women in the society, by empowering them through higher education. (For more details on this special message, please see para 7.13).

(xiv) At the time of elections, or when selection is made for filling important positions, only those candidates should be supported who are enthusiastic about promoting world peace.

(xv) Full support should be given to government programs which seek to maintain self-defence capability—keeping in mind the fact that such capability depends jointly on military strength, and a feeling of unity among the people brought about by non-discriminatory policies of the government. (For more details on this special message, please see para 7.15).

(xvi) Full support should be given to the following: Whatever disputes a country might have with the governments of other countries, its government should take a firm policy decision to settle them peacefully, because wars cannot provide a satisfactory solution to any dispute. (For more details on this special message, please see para 7.16).

(xvii) No support should be given to the idea of any one having a private army, because all military should be under the direct control of the government. (For more details on this special message, please see para 7.17).

(xviii) No donation or help or support of any kind should be given to anti-social elements which are likely to disturb world peace. (For details please see para 7.18).

(xix) Religious leaders should not only give a free hand to the younger generation for embarking on a peace-initiative, but should also become a part of that movement. (For more details on this special message, please see para 7.20 where the peace-initiative is called 'Shanti-yajna' which is defined as follows: A person can be called a performer of 'Shanti-yajna', if he or she considers world peace as the goal of dharma (religion), if his or her talks are centered on world peace, if world peace is the aim of his or her education, and if he or she teaches world peace to others too—in short, if all the activities are centered on world peace).

(xx) Religious leaders should take part in inter-faith dialogues, enthusiastically, so that such dialogues could be held in an increasing number of places, and a written statement on 'How to establish inter-religious harmony' could be produced by them. (For more details on this special message, please see para 7.21).

(xxi) Religious leaders should remember that their predecessors were advised by the creator to teach common people about lokasamgraha (good of all), hoping that the chain of such teaching will never be broken. Such teaching will help the cause of world peace because lokasamgraha and world peace go together. (For more details on this special message, please see para 7.22).

(xxii) Religious leaders should remember that their predecessors set in motion the policy of Svadharma (i.e. the right to choose one's faith freely) with the hope that the same policy will be continued. Therefore, no support should be given to anyone who attempts to obtain conversion of faith by offering financial or other benefit. (For more details on this special message, please see para 7.23).

(xxiii) Religious leaders should remember that King Janaka welcomed Sulabha, the saintly lady, and fully supported women's right to function as a spiritual leader. The twenty-first century demands that the scope of women's rights should be further widened. (For more details on this special message, please see para 7.24).

(xxiv) Full support should be given to war-ravaged sections of the society in their attempt to gather support for world peace. (For more details on this special message, please see para 8.22).

(xxv) Vegetarian societies and other groups collaborating with them, should be given full freedom to carry on their publicity against meat-eating. (For more details on this special message, please see para 8.25).

(xxvi) Non-violent activists should be given full freedom to carry on their publicity in support of world peace.

(xxvii) Writers and journalists (or media people in general) should be encouraged to record and popularize the contributions that ordinary persons (men, women and children) are making all the time to the cause of world peace, in different countries. (For more details on this special message, please see paras 8.26 and 8.27).

(xxviii) Full support should be given (in countries where this message is applicable), to any proposal which seeks to replace, by peaceful means, a dictatorial form of government, by a democratic set-up, because such a change would be conducive to world peace. (For more details on this special message, please see para 5.36).

(xxix) Full support should be given to any proposal which seeks to establish, by peaceful means, a secular democratic set-up in any country (where this message is applicable), because a theocratic set-up at home is less likely to promote world peace, as compared to a secular set-up. (For more details on this special message, please see paras 3.15 and 5.23).

Category three: Messages to be considered by governments of different countries

9.5. Before we summarize the messages of this category, we want to draw attention to our main recommendation in regard to governments of different countries (all of which, as members of the UN, are supposed to contribute to the cause of world peace), that they should strengthen their commitment to world peace by preparing a WPPP (World Peace Promotion Preparedness) Index with the help of a self-administered check-list. Items included in the check-list are essentially the messages given by the Mahabharata to the governments for their consideration (mainly presented in chapter six). The total number of messages is twenty-five, and the WPPP Index for any government is the percentage of those messages to which that government is prepared to give a 'yes' reply. The sequence of presentation of the messages is broadly the same as suggested by the Mahabharata—in fact, the messages are similar to the ones already given above in categories one and two:

(i) The government should give no legal sanction or silent authorization to any one who may be planning to commit suicide. For the twenty-first century, this message means that suicide bombers do not receive the slightest approval from the government—rather, the disapproval of the government should be widely publicized.

(ii) The government should give no support (direct or indirect) to any one who may be planning to ignore his or her social responsibilities (which include the maintenance of world peace). In other words, world peace-breakers should know that their anti-social activities have no governmental support.

(iii) No governmental support of any kind should be given to those who scoff at other people's faith (through cartoons, for example).

(iv) The government should ban discrimination based on faith, sex, race, colour, language, country of residence, etc.

(v) Strong governmental support should be given to programs which are meant to help those who are orphans, oppressed, or too weak to take care of themselves. (Sympathy for such persons may create the desire to avoid violence or war, which aggravates this type of problems, both in one's own country and also in another country).

(vi) Strong governmental support should be given to programs which are meant to honor old people or which seek to make special arrangements to satisfy their health and psychological needs.

(vii) Strong governmental support should be given to programs which seek to make necessary adjustments or changes in traditional concepts, to keep pace with changes in time, place and circumstances. (To put an end to historical animosities is one such program, and these messages contain more such programs).

(viii) Strong governmental support should be given to programs which seek to give the right education to all the children (i.e. boys as well as girls), and which seek to use education to cultivate right values in the society (including the strengthening of fellow-feeling among the people following different faiths). The government should officially declare that one of the aims of education will be to prepare the minds of students so that they become fit to be peace-loving citizens of the world. In pursuance of this aim, all the students will be given broad-based education and they will also be taught how to use their knowledge for the benefit of mankind. Such teaching should also emphasize and ensure that no student will use his or her knowledge to destroy world peace. If necessary, the Government may seek technical assistance from UNESCO so that they can plan for all-round educational development, and also implement such plans as quickly and smoothly as possible.

(ix) The government should further widen the scope of educational reform programs so that they cover not only the school-age children but also the adults. (For more details on this special message, please see para 8.11)

(x) The government should prepare, as well as support, programs which seek to increase food production in the country, as also to increase employment opportunities in socially useful jobs, and which seek to make all the people healthy and prosperous. (Increasing employment opportunities in the military for aggressive purposes is not covered in this message).

(xi) The government should prepare programs which seek to protect the environment, for example, by planting and protecting trees. (Damage to environment is particularly severe due to war).

(xii) The government should prepare programs which seek to raise the status of women in the society, by empowering them through higher education. (For more details on this special message, please see para 6.22)

(xiii) The government should prepare a well-balanced program which seeks to maintain self-defence capability - keeping in mind the fact that such capability depends jointly on military strength, and a feeling of unity among the people brought about by its non-discriminatory policies. (For more details on this special message, please see para 6.24).

(xiv) Whatever disputes a country might have with the governments of other countries, its government should take a firm policy decision to settle them peacefully, because wars cannot provide a satisfactory solution to any dispute. (For more details on this special message, please see para 6.25).

(xv) The government should strongly disapprove the idea of any one having a private army, because all military should be under the control of the government. Similarly, no one should be allowed by the government to use its territory for anti-social and peace-breaking activities. (For more details on this special message, please see paras 6.26 and 6.27).

(xvi) The government should ensure that no donation or help or support of any kind is given to anti-social elements which are likely to disturb world peace. (For details please see para 6.27).

(xvii) The government should ensure that its ministers and advisers are committed to peace. Particularly, the officials of the External Affairs Ministry should be sent to attend a course on "Techniques of Conflict Resolution"-such courses are currently offered by several universities in USA and other countries.

(xviii) Although inter-faith dialogues are primarily the responsibility of religious leaders, the government should act as a catalyst to set in motion such dialogues in an increasing number of places, and also to facilitate the production of a written statement on 'How to establish inter-religious harmony' as one of the outcomes of such dialogues. (For more details on this special message, please see para 7.21).

(xix) Although a peace initiative by the youth (called by the Mahabharata as Shanti-yajna) is primarily the responsibility of NGO's, the government should act as a catalyst to ensure that such a bold initiative meets no stiff resistance. (For more details on this special message, please see para 7.20)

(xx) The government should give full freedom to non-violent activists for carrying on their publicity in support of world peace.

(xxi) The government should give full freedom to war-ravaged sections of the society for trying to gather support for world peace. (For more details on this special message, please see para 8.22).

(xxii) The government should give full freedom to vegetarian societies and other groups collaborating with them, for carrying on their publicity against meat-eating. (For more details on this special message, please see para 8.25).

(xxiii) Writers and journalists (or media people in general) should be encouraged by the Government to record and popularize the contributions that ordinary persons (men, women and children) are making all the time to the cause of world peace, in different countries. (For more details on this special message, please see paras 8.26 and 8.27).

(xxiv) Full support should be given by the government (in countries where this message is applicable) to any proposal which seeks to replace, by peaceful means, a dictatorial form of government, by a democratic set-up, because such a change would be conducive to world peace. (For more details on this special message, please see para 5.36).

(xxv) Full support should be given by the government to any proposal which seeks to establish, by peaceful means, a secular democratic set-up in any country (where this message is applicable), because a theocratic set-up at home is less likely to promote world peace, as compared to a secular set-up. (For more details on this special message, please see paras 3.15 and 5.23).

Category four: Messages to be considered by UNESCO

9.6. Although the Mahabharata could not possibly envisage that UNESCO would be established in the world in the twentieth century, its (i.e. Mahabharata's) messages for this category can be derived from the suggestions that assign a very important role to education, in bringing about world peace (reference para 5.21). UNESCO's own approach to this issue, as summarized in its famous statement "Since wars begin in the minds of men, it is in the minds of men that the defences of peace must be constructed", is thus essentially similar to the Mahabharata's. For purposes of summarization, we want to draw attention to four messages:

(i) The main contribution of UNESCO in the twenty-first century, according to this book, could be to convince all the governments of the world that they should declare world peace to be one of the aims of education in their respective country. Specifically, the aim of education everywhere, should be declared to be "To prepare the minds of students so that they become fit to be peace-loving citizens of the world". In pursuance of this aim, all the students of the world should be taught how to use their knowledge for the benefit of mankind. In other words, the educational process everywhere should emphasize and ensure that no student will use his or her knowledge to destroy world peace. UNESCO should be ready to give technical assistance to those countries which might be unable to achieve, by themselves, all that is outlined in this para. (For more details on this special message, please see para 8.11).

(ii) All peace-destroying (and hatred-causing) components of the education system (public, private or religious, in whichever part of the world they might exist) should be modified, improved, or discontinued, in the interest of world peace. UNESCO would be the most appropriate agency of UN to be able to achieve this, which is a difficult but important task, preparatory to world peace.

(iii) UNESCO may consider designating selected universities in the world as "Peace Universities" (or Shanti-Niketan, in the words of Tagore—reference para 3.10), which would have adequate facilities for:

(a) Teaching comparative religion (from the perspective of bringing about inter-religious harmony).

(b) Teaching a course on "Techniques of Conflict Resolution".

(c) Training teachers (both men and women) deputed by different countries, in the above-mentioned special fields, so that they (i.e. teachers) would return to their own country to teach the same subjects.

(iv) UNESCO may consider the possibility of functioning as a catalyst, for establishing inter-cultural communities like Auroville in different parts of the world, to promote the cause of inter-cultural understanding and world peace. (For more details on this special message, please see para 4.52).

Category five: Messages to be considered by the United Nations

9.7. Messages in this category are intended to strengthen the UN by gathering mass support for it, while it tackles the difficult problem of establishing world peace. But first, why should we expect the UN to pay any attention to what this book says ? Two considerations have created in us the desire to put forth a couple of suggestions. Primarily, the immense practical wisdom (relating to peace) contained in Shanti-Parva of the Mahabharata, gives enormous weight to our suggestions, because scholars from all over the world have recognized that the Mahabharata contains messages (essentially non-denominational) which have the potential to contribute to the good of mankind, even in the twenty-first century. Secondly, as peace-loving citizens of the world who have worked (in technical advisory capacity) with a Specialized Agency (International Labour Office) of the UN, in different countries for many years, we feel the urge to offer suggestions which have already been discussed by us at an international conference on world peace held at the University of Houston, Houston, Texas, USA in July 2006. Having thus given the background to our heart-felt move, we offer below two suggestions for consideration by the United Nations:

(i) The UN should make the peace process a mass movement. It should designate 24th October as "World Peace Day", and obtain the approval of all the governments to the effect that 'World Peace Day' will be celebrated in all the countries, by educational institutions (with full participation of students), as well as by women's organizations and other non-governmental groups. During the rest of the year too, different types of peaceful functions (as determined by local people), in support of world peace, should be held.

(ii) The UN should initiate a research and discussion process for gradually enhancing what we have called the 'World Peace Promotion Preparedness' of selected governments (after giving the assurance that this selection is done objectively, without any bias). The Mahabharata has stressed that the contribution of any government to the cause of world peace largely depends on the qualitative composition and internal policies of that government. For example, the contribution to world peace, of a dictatorial type of government (which may not attach much importance to human rights) is likely to be less than that of a democratic government. Similarly, the contribution to world peace, of a theocratic form of government (which may not show equal respect to all the faiths) is likely to be less than that of a secular government. We have presented under category three above (i.e. para 9.5), a self- administered check-list of twenty-five items, on the basis of which each government can calculate the value of WPPP (World Peace Promotion Preparedness) Index for itself—the index is the percentage of items in this checklist for which the government is prepared to give a 'yes' reply. After considering all the points carefully, the UN could give a final shape to this check-list (our draft is given in para 9.5, and therefore not repeated here), by adding other questions (like the nuclear question about which the Mahabharata could not possibly have thought of). Once such a procedure is set in motion, the UN could then put invisible pressure on the governments with a relatively lower WPPP Index, to find out ways of raising that Index in the years to come. Delicate issues which cannot by themselves be easily raised with the various governments, form a part of WPPP Index, therefore we feel confident that this approach (modified if necessary) will be found by UN to serve a useful, practical purpose i.e. accelerating the rate of progress to the goal of world peace.

Concluding remarks

9.8. What sort of follow-up action should we expect or try for, on the messages contained in this book? With a view to arousing all-round interest which may prompt such action, we want to draw attention to five points :

(a) The messages are so comprehensive that every person or institution will find in them, something of interest, because one of our main suggestions to UN is, to make the peace process a mass movement and to invite everyone to contribute new ideas (reference para 9.7).

(b) The messages envisage a crucial role for education, which must prepare the minds of students (boys as well as girls) all over the world so that they become fit to be peace-loving citizens of the world (reference para 9.6).

(c) The messages pin their hope on the younger generation for embarking on a peace initiative (the Mahabharata's expression is 'Shanti-yajna', a significant word implying strong commitment, and participation of all) (reference para 7.20).

(d) For strengthening the commitment of the various

governments to world peace, we have suggested the use of a new Index, viz. the WPPP (World Peace Promotion Preparedness) Index. This is the technological modernization of the Mahabharata's ideas, to make them appropriate and applicable to the twenty-first century (reference paras 9.5 and 9.7).

(e) The fact that the above messages (and many more) have been derived from the Mahabharata, does not mean that they represent only the Indian point of view. If read with an open mind, the messages will be found to be universal. For example, the Mahabharata's explicitly anti-war message can be considered by all the governments: "Whatever disputes a government might have with the governments of other countries, it should take a firm policy decision to settle them peacefully, because wars cannot provide a satisfactory solution to any dispute" (reference para 6.25).

9.9. To facilitate follow-up action, we have classified the messages into five categories, each of which can be considered, almost independently, by:

(i) Common people of the world and NGO's
(ii) Religious leaders of different faiths
(iii) Governments of different countries
(iv) UNESCO
(v) UN

It is hoped that plenty of purposeful discussion (with an open mind) will be held all over the world, to arrive at new proposals which can help bring world peace within the reach of mankind, in the twenty-first century.

9.10. Since the messages contained in this book are based on an innovative research project,we hope the academic community will take special interest in looking at them. (For their benefit, we have given the Sanskrit text, in devanagari as well as Roman script). We realize that some of the scholars (in the past) found the Mahabharata to be "too long", and rather difficult to be classified as an "epic" when standards laid down in Europe were applied to it. However, we now hope that technical considerations of this type have not created a long-lasting bias against an ancient text which has so much to offer. At any rate, there should be no lack of enthusiasm in studying the messages which have been derived from the Shanti-Parva section of the Mahabharata and are presented here in a simplified form. It is hoped that this book will arouse afresh the interest of scholars in Shanti-Parva, which is practically a book by itself, containing so many messages of peace that are relevant even today. Of course, the style of conveying the messages (for example, telling a story) may be unfamiliar to some. But to a patient reader, to go through these stories on a selective basis will definitely prove to be rewarding. Specifically, the remarkable story of a young scholar and peace-promoter, Medhavi (which we have summarized in para 7.20) is worth the effort needed to locate it, out of a large number of stories. We should be grateful to the author of the Mahabharata for having narrated this story twice (thus giving a hint about its importance), and we should de-emphasize the technical flaw involved in repeating the same story (which is one of the reasons why the Mahabharata seems to some to be too long).

9.11. In the recently published book "The Mahabharata: What is not here is nowhere else", the Editor, T.S. Rukmani, makes the following, encouraging remark (which implies that our hope of arousing scholars, interest in Shanti-Parva, as expressed in the preceding para, has a bright chance of getting fulfilled):

"The critical edition of the Mahabharata brought out by the Bhandarkar Oriental Research Institute, Pune, is a milestone in the history of Mahabharata scholarship which has since driven a number of innovative research in the vast treasures of this *itihasa* all round the world. From viewing the Mahabharata as a 'monstrous mass of songs' in the past, for instance, it has widened the lens, and scholars are now more interested in looking for answers for specific questions that beset all humans that live in this complex world. The approach now is not that the Mahabharata is a culture-specific text applicable only to the Indian context as such but that the text is indeed engaged in portraying the complexities and dilemmas that each one of us faces in the lived world. These is no other text, perhaps, more suited to guide humans in this difficult task of engaging oneself in the world specially in these troubled times, than the Mahabharata itself."[1]

9.12. Non-availability of a suitable English translation of Shanti-Parva is certainly a problem which scholars have faced, because even the famous rendering by K.M.Ganguli (accomplished during the years 1883-1896) has not done justice to the lokasamgraha-related portion which is so important for deriving the peace-messages. (Ganguli himself has admitted in his Preface that he found the Shanti-Parva to be most difficult). We hope Nicholas Sutton's work involving translation of parts of Shanti-Parva will help solve the problem to some extent.

9.13. In the end, we would like to quote, rather extensively, Nicholas Sutton's opinion (expressed in his book "Religious Doctrines in the Mahabharata" published in the year 2000) about the "potential contribution" that the Mahabharata can make to global issues, if it is read with an unbiased mind:

"It is perhaps inappropriate to attempt an evaluation of the Mahabharata, for any such judgements are inevitably subjective and culturally conditioned. Traditional Christianity has a deep-seated interest in denegrating the ideas and practices of other traditions in order to establish the uniqueness of its own revelation, whilst post-enlightenment Western thought regards sequential reasoning as the absolute key to knowledge, and judges pejoratively any work that does not mirror this view. Hence any evaluation of the epic from the West, however closely reasoned, is almost inevitably an ethno-centric judgement based on culturally derived preconceptions. Perhaps it is sufficient to recognize the Mahabharata as a great classic of religious literature and I hope the present study has served somewhat to demonstrate an aspect of this greatness by highlighting its potential contribution to a global theology, and the profundity of its reflection on the deepest questions that humanity faces generation after generation."[2]

Notes

Chapter 1

1. The international conference on world peace was organized by WAVES (World Association for Vedic Studies), and held at the University of Houston, Houston, Texas, USA on 8-10 July 2006. The chairman of the conference, Dr. S.N. Dwivedi, assigned to the author of this book, the task of organizing and conducting a session on 'Practical Steps to World Peace'. Besides this, the author also presented a paper on 'Mahabharata's Message of World Peace'.
2. The ten publications (all brought out by Motilal Banarsidass) are: The Social Role of the Gita, The Social Message of the Gita Symbolized as Lokasamgraha, Tulasi Ramayana: Jagmangal-Parayan, Manas evam Gita: Lokmangal-Gunjita, Lokasamgrahasandesh, The Gita and Tulsi-Ramayana: Their Common Call for the Good of All. The Gita for the Twenty-first Century, Chhatropayogi Bhagavad Gita, Shrimad-Bhagwat Ka Gyan: Din-dukhi ki Seva Mahan, and Selections from the Mahabharata: Reaffirming Gita's Call for the Good of All.

Chapter 2

1. Rabindranath Tagore, Gitanjali, UBS Publishers, New Delhi, 2005, p.36.
2. S. Radhakrishnan and C.A. Moore, A Sourcebook in Indian Philosophy, Princeton University Press, 1973, p.5.
3. Satya P. Agarwal, The Social Message of the Gita Symbolized as Lokasamgraha, Motilal Banarsidass, Delhi, 1995, p.78.
4. Rabindranath Tagore, Gitanjali, op. cit., p.35.

CHAPTER 3

1. S. Radhakrishnan and C.A. Moore, A Sourcebook in Indian Philosophy, op.cit., p.39.
2. There are four Mahavakyas in the Upanisads, one each in Aitareya Upanisad, Brihadaranyak Upanisad, Chandogya Upanisad, and Mandukya Upanisad. All of them give the message of oneness of all human beings.
3. Swami Vivekananda, Complete Works, eight volumes, Advaita Ashrama, Calcutta, fourteenth edition, 1972, Vol.I, pp. 4 and 11.
4. Rabindranath Tagore's poem "Old and New" is not included in Gitanjali. The author is grateful to Himendra Thakur for sending him a copy of the poem.
5. Swami Ranganathananda, The Message of the Upanisads, Bharatiya Vidya Bhawan, Bombay, 1971, p.44.
6. Ibid., p.20
7. Rabindranath Tagore, Gitanjali, op.cit, pp. 299-300.
8. Raghavan Iyer, The Moral and Political Thought of Mahatma Gandhi, Oxford University Press, New York, 1978, p.326.
9. V.P. Verma, The Political Philosophy of Mahatma Gandhi and Sarvodaya, Laxmi Narain, Agra, 1959, p.59.
10. Jawaharlal Nehru, The Discovery of India, Meridian Books Limited, London, 1947, p.303.
11. Swami Ranganathananda, The Message of the Upanisads, op.cit., p.38.
12. Satya P. Agarwal, The Social Role of the Gita, Motilal Banarsidass, 1993, p.178.

CHAPTER 4

1. Mahadev Desai, The Gita according to Gandhi, Navajivan Publishing House, Ahmedabad, 2004, pp. 131-32.
2. Swami Vivekananda, Complete Works, Vol. I, pp. 4, 17-18.
3. Satya P. Agarwal, The Social Message of the Gita Symbolized as Lokasamgraha, pp. 78-86.

4. Stanley A. Wolpert, Tilak and Gokhale: Revolution and Reform in the Making of Modern India, University of California Press, 1962, p. 191.
5. B.G. Tilak, Gita-Rahasya. Tilak Brothers, Poona, 1975, p.713.
6. Sri Aurobindo, Essays on the Gita, New York edition, 1950, p. 122.
7. Robert Mc Dermott (ed.), The Essential Aurobindo, Schocken Books, New York, 1973, p. 240.
8. Madeleine Biardeau, Hinduism: The Anthology of a Civilization. Oxford University Press, Delhi, 1989, pp.164-65.
9. P.M. Thomas, 20th Century Indian Interpretations of Bhagavad Gita: Tilak, Gandhi and Aurobindo, Christian Institute for the Study of Religion and Society, Bangalore, 1987, pp. 202-3.
10. Ibid., p. 203.

Chapter 5

1. Nicholas Sutton, Religious Doctrines in the Mahabharata, Motilal Banarsidass, Delhi, 2000, pp. 307-8.
2. Ramkinkar Upadhyay, A Comparative Study of Manas and Gita (in Hindi), Tulsi Tattvanusandhan Kendra, Kanpur, 1987, pp. 143-52.
3. For details, see Satya P. Agarwal, Selections from the Mahabharata, Motilal Banarsidass, Delhi, 2002.
4. Arvind Sharma, Hinduism for our Times, Oxford University Press, Delhi, 1996, p. 28.
5. Swami Vivekananda, Complete Works, Vol.I, pp. 68-70.

Chapter 6

1. Mahadev Desai, The Gita according to Gandhi, pp. 128-33.

Chapter 7

1. For more details, see Satya P. Agarwal, Selections from the Mahabharata, pp. 163-70.

Chapter 8

1. Barend A. van Nooten, The Mahabharata attributed to Krishna Dvaipayana Vyas, Twayne Publishers, New York, 1971, p. 7.

Chapter 9

1. T.S. Rukmani, The Mahabharata: What is not here is nowhere else, Munshiram Manoharlal, New Delhi, 2005, p. xvii.
2. Nicholas Sutton, Religious Doctrines in the Mahabharata, pp. 461-62.

Index

References are to paragraph numbers, not to pages

L

M

N

O

P

R

-: BY THE SAME AUTHOR :-

The Gītā for the Twenty-First Century: Bhagavad Gītā Universal Message—This latest version of Bhagavad Gītā (with ślokas in Sanskrit and commentary in English) explains how the message of social service has been derived from this universal scripture.

ISBN: 81-7822-153-5 *Rs. 195*

The Gītā and Tulasī-Rāmāyaṇa: Their Common Call for the Good of All—This book has identified "the good of all" as the single most important criterion of excellence of any socio-spiritual approach to life's problems—particularly in the context of the conflict-ridden society of today.

ISBN: 81-208-1752-4 *Rs. 295*

The Social Role of the Gītā How & Why—The present work is a new perspective on the *Bhagavad-Gītā,* supported by thorough research, for it focuses attention on the social relevance of this famous Hindu scripture.

ISBN: 81-208-1524-6 *Rs. 225*

The Social Message of the Gītā: Symbolized as Lokasaṁgraha —This book is a landmark in the wide panorama of Gita literature, the universal nature of which is reflected in the use—in the form of prose as well as poetry—of an increasing number of the world's languages.

ISBN: 81-208-1319-7 *Rs. 275*

Selections from the Mahābhārata: Re-affirming Gītā's Call for the Good of All—This book presents the social message of the Mahābhārata in the form of a ten-point call for the good of all.

ISBN: 81-208-1874-1 *$19.95*

तुलसी रामायण जगमंगल-परायण रू० 295

मानस एवं गीता लोकमंगल-गुञ्जिता रू० 295